The Sidhe

Wisdom from the Celtic Otherworld

Also by John Matthews

The Arthurian Tarot: A Hallowquest (with Caitlin Matthews)
Aquarian Press, 1990
Bardic Source Book *Cassell, 1998*
Book of Arthur *Vega, 2002*
Celtic Seers Source-Book *Cassell, 1999*
The Celtic Shaman *Element, 1991*
The Celtic Shaman's Pack (ill. Chesca Potter) *Element, 1996*
Celtic Totem Animals *Eddison Sadd/Red Wheel, 2002*
Classic Celtic Faery Tales *Cassell, 1996*
Drinking From the Sacred Well *Harper San Francisco, 1999*
Druid Source-Book *Cassell, 1996*
The Encyclopaedia of Celtic Wisdom: A Celtic Shaman's
Sourcebook *Rider Books, 2001*
The Faery Tale Reader (with Caitlin Matthews) *Aquarian, 1993*
From the Hollow Hills *Floris Books, 1994.*
From the Isle of Dreams *Floris Books, 1993.*
Gawain, Knight of the Goddess Inner Traditions, *2003*
The Grail: Quest for the Eternal Thames & Hudson, *1981*
Healing the Wounded King *Element, 1997*
Ladies of the Lake (with Caitlin Matthews) *Aquarian Press, 1992*
Malory's Mort D'Arthur (ED) *Orion, 2000*
Merlin Through the Ages (with R.J.Stewart) *Cassell, 1995*
Quest for the Green Man *Godsfield Press/Quest Books, 2000*
Song of Arthur *Quest Books, 2002*
Song of Taliesin *Quest Books, 2001*
Sources of the Grail *Floris Books, 1996*
Taliesin: the Last Celtic Shaman *Aquarian, 1991/Inner Traditions,
2002*
Walkers Between Worlds (with Caitlin Matthews) *Inner
Traditions, 2003*
Warriors of Arthur (with Bob Stewart) *Blandford Press, 1987*
The Winter Solstice *Godsfield Press, 1997*

The Sidhe

Wisdom from the Celtic Otherworld

John Matthews

The Lorian Press
2204 E Grand Ave.
Everett, WA 98201
www.lorian.org

Edited by Susan Sherman and Dana Standish

Cover painting by Deva Berg
Great Glyph inside illustration by Valorie Fanger

Published by The Lorian Press
2204 E Grand Ave.
Everett, WA 98201

ISBN   0-936878-05-3

Matthews, John
The Sidhe / John Matthews

Library of Congress Control Number: 2004093539

First Edition: May 2004 - Second Edition: October 2007

Printed in the United States of America

9 8 7 6 5 4 3 2 1 0

www.lorian.org

Dedication

To the People of the Sidhe
And to the intrepid members of the Jean Houston
Tour of Britain 2000
Who first heard some of these words read aloud and responded
so positively to them.

JM. Oxford, 2004.

THE SIDHE

Wisdom from the Celtic Otherworld

Table of Contents

Preface

Many of the words you are about to read were dictated to me by beings that only I could see. Every day for several weeks I sat at my computer, eyes half closed, occasionally glancing up at the image pinned up above my desk. Then, for a space, I would type furiously, fingers attempting to keep up with the words I was hearing. The beings who communicated with me in this way called themselves the *Sidhe*, an ancient name for the faery race of Ireland. I had and have no reason to disbelieve them, since the evidence of my inner senses assured me they were as real as I (presumably) am. What they had to say seems both fascinating and even at times profound, and is certainly not the product of my own imagination.

Some people will perceive this as a 'channeled' book, and may well recall that, over the years, I have not always had positive things to say about channeling. A great deal of the material produced through this means still seems, to me, at best unreliable and at worst misleading. For this reason alone I thought a great deal before I decided to set down this account—let alone publish it. In the end it was a combination of two things—friendly pressure from colleagues, together with the nature of the material, what was actually being said, that persuaded me. Not that I believe what is set down here to be any more important than information contained in a dozen other books representing the words of the faery races, but rather that what is contained here may well have value for others on the spiritual path. So, I have decided to tell the story more or less as it happened, and without further explanation, leaving it to the minds and hearts of those who read it to decide whether it has any merit for them.

For obvious reasons I have changed names and locations, and the frame for the words dictated to me by the Sidhe has been cast in the form of a story to make it more readable. There is no site called Gortnasheen in Ireland, though the place where the events described here does exist.

I should like to thank Keith Harris (not his real name) for inviting me on what was to become the most exciting journey of my life. Also thanks to Jeremy Berg at the Lorian Press for his willingness to take on this project, to my wife Caitlin for asking the right questions at the right time and to my friend David Spangler for adding to them.

But my deepest debt is to the people of the Sidhe, themselves, who have so much to teach us still, even in the twenty-first century.

J.M. England and USA - 2003

Chapter One
The Call To Ireland

"I have things to say that should be heard by
your people."

The phone was ringing as I came in from the rainy streets of Oxford. I dropped my bag and hurried to pick up.

"Hello, John? This is Keith—Keith Harris. From Dublin. I think I've got something that might interest you."

I ran through the address book in my head and came up with a match. Keith Harris was an archaeologist working for the Irish Heritage Board. His specific responsibility was ancient monuments.

"Hello, Keith. Good to hear from you. What's up?"

"It's a new site. Just west of Dungarrow. We've been digging there for the past year. Found a few interesting things. Thought you might like to come and do a piece on it."

I make a living from the study of ancient history and traditions, especially as these have to do with the native lands of Britain and Ireland. I have taught these things in Britain and the United States, and have written numerous books about them. This has led to some friendships with archaeologists who keep an open mind on such matters. Keith was one such, and more than once had brought me in to look at some intriguing sites.

I thought hard, trying to remember anything I had heard about places in the area Keith had named.

"It's good of you to think of me, " I said at last. "What can you tell me about this place?"

"Nothing right now. I'd rather wait till you get here."

"Sounds mysterious."

"Not really. I just don't want to commit myself till I'm sure. Are you interested?"

"When would you want me to come out?"

"No special rush. As soon as it's convenient."

I looked at the calendar, which was, truth to tell, somewhat bare at the moment. The day was the 6th of July, 1998.

"OK. I'll be there on Friday."

"Great. I'll meet you at the airport. See you in three days."

He rang off and I put the phone down. An hour later, sitting at my desk, I found myself thinking about the call, wondering just what there was at this newly discovered site. A strange feeling came over me as I did so. It was a kind I had felt before. Some people would call it a

2

"psychic prickle." I sometimes get it when I visit certain ancient sites. It is as though the people who had lived there once were trying to speak to me. Sometimes I even believed I heard voices, but generally I kept quiet about this for obvious reasons. I had a "name" as an expert on historical themes. Suggesting that I have psychic contact with people who have been dead for several hundred years is not a good idea in my line of work, and this has made me hesitate a good deal before publishing this account.

But the "prickle" was there—like a cold finger across the nape of my neck. I knew then that something was going to happen in Ireland. I had no idea then just what an enormous and irrevocable change it was going to make to my life.

Three days later I got off the plane at Dublin airport and was met by Keith Harris. He shook my hand warmly.

"Welcome to Ireland, John."

Keith looked more like a farmer than an archaeologist. He was short and stockily built with a face reddened by days spent in the open. He was about sixty years of age but looked younger, his bright blue eyes still full of youthful enthusiasm.

"Sorry about all the mystification," he said as we walked to his battered old car. "It's just that there's something about the site at Gortnasheen that's, well, different."

That was the first time I heard the name. Even then, before I had seen the place, I once again felt the "prickle" of a feeling I could not account for with any usual reason. I said nothing at the time, preferring to wait and allow events to unfold.

After this one remark Keith studiously avoided the topic of his latest dig, preferring, as we drove out of the sprawl of Dublin and into the rich green land to the west, to confine himself to general topics such as what I had been doing since we had last met (at a very dull party honoring a very dull colleague, we decided) almost three years before. Of his own activities he spoke only of the excavations at other interesting sites currently being carried out under the aegis of the Irish Heritage Board. But though I listened, and responded as was appropriate, my thoughts were all of Gortnasheen and what might be awaiting me there. Somehow, though I could not have explained it if I had tried, I knew that what I was going to find was far more than a tumble of rocks or an archaeological trench.

The drive from Dublin to the site took a little over two hours. The landscape through which we traveled was mostly low lying, a richly undulating carpet of green. It had been grey and overcast when I arrived, but as we motored west the sky began to clear and soon a watery sun emerged. Keith commented on the fact that this was the first day it had stopped raining for nearly a week ("It's not made our work any easier!") then fell silent as we drove the last few miles to the small village of Dungarrow, the nearest habitation to the site of the dig.

Once there, Keith checked me into the local pub and suggested we both get something to eat before going on to the site. I felt a sudden reluctance on his part, as though, having brought me this far, he was beginning to wonder if he had done the right thing.

Over a plate of fish and chips and a pint of the best ale, I decided to tackle the subject head on.

"Tell me about the site," I ventured.

Keith took another sip of beer, then set the glass down on the table, perhaps just a bit too firmly. "If you don't mind, I'd rather not say anything until you've seen the place," he said at last. As he did so I thought his cheeks grew even redder than usual, and he was definitely reluctant to look at me.

"Good grief, what have you got there, buried treasure?" I asked lightly.

"What! No, nothing like that," Keith said. Finally, he did meet my eyes. "Look. I'm really sorry about all this. You must think I've lost it. It's just that...." he hesitated, then finished in a rush. "Well, it's a feeling, nothing I can really explain. I just don't want to feed in any preconceived ideas...."

It was on the tip of my tongue to say that all the mystery was doing just that, but I decided instead to keep silent.

We finished our lunch without further discussion, then got back into Keith's car and drove away from the village, following the winding road until it became a track and, when even that petered out, a rutted field. Finally, when I thought that either my body or Keith's ancient vehicle was going to give up the ghost, we came to a stop.

Keith sat for a moment before he turned off the engine. Then he turned to me, his face serious.

"Look, I'm not at all sure why I brought you here," he blurted. "The truth is—and I know it's going to sound daft—I dreamed about you three nights in a row. I'd been trying to think of the best person to come and look at what we found here, and quite honestly your name wasn't on the list. But after those dreams I started to think about something you said to me ages ago—how some of these old sites seemed more alive than others. At the time I didn't really understand what you meant—in fact, I probably thought you were a bit mad. But there's something about this place... well, you'll see for yourself in a moment..." He trailed off, looking at me with more than a touch of desperation.

"Let's go then, "I said, opening my door, not wanting to commit myself to anything more. "You can tell me about the site as we go." I had already peered out of the window across the field and could see nothing.

Keith produced two pairs of Wellington boots and we set off across the soft earth of the field.

"Most of what we've found inside is neolithic, dating from around 2000 BC," said Keith, with evident relief to be talking about familiar territory. "But there's also later material, from about 200 BC, the time of the Celts. The current theory is that the site was in use for around eight hundred years after that. But it's definitely much older, at a guess I'd say as much as four thousand years."

"So, we're looking at a Stone Age site? One that was used by the Celts some time after that?"

Keith nodded. "The real question is, used for what?" he added.

I stopped in mid stride. "You mean, you don't know?" It was such an odd statement from a leading archaeologist. Normally they were so full of ideas and opinions as to the purpose of any site they were working on.

Keith hesitated before he answered. "It's not as simple as that. On the face of it it's a straightforward enough site. What concerns me are the differences from the norm. But look, here we are, I'll leave it to you to decide what you think."

We turned into another field, passing through a hedge. There before us was what looked like a scattered pile of boulders, ranging in size from massive to head sized. To the casual eye they appeared to be no more than that, but I had visited enough such sites to recognize the unmistakable signs of human construction.

5

In fact the stones were not as scattered as they first appeared. Rather they seemed to erupt from the ground, in places still half buried, while others had fallen sideways out of what I now saw was a roughly oblong mound. As we walked around it, I saw the indications of the archaeological work that had been going on there: areas of turf stripped back, a long trench about two feet wide and six feet deep running off at right angles to the mound.

Then we came round to what I knew to be the western end of the mound, and I saw that between two particularly massive stones was a low, oblong space opening into darkness. This was clearly the entrance. It had been roped off and a roughly written sign hung from the line. The sign read:

PRIVATE PROPERTY
KEEP OUT

Keith stepped forward and lifted the rope out of the way.

"What I want you to see is inside" he said. You'll find a torch on the ledge just inside."

As I stood in front of the entrance to the mound the feeling I had experienced twice before returned — only this time it was twice as strong. At that moment had a figure from any period of time but the present stepped out of the mound, I would not have been at all surprised. The sense of timeless energy emanating from the dark hole was such that I actually thought I could not move at all. Then, just as suddenly as it had come, the feeling passed. Crouching down, I peered into the hole.

A waft of cold air struck my face — something that might have struck me as odd if I had been thinking about it — normally such sites were not very deep or extensive underground and the chances of air being trapped inside were slight. But, I confess that I was not thinking about such things at all. I felt a rising tide of excitement as I inched forward into the darkness, feeling rough stone on all sides and fumbling for the ledge and the torch.

6

I found them easily enough and in a moment the wide, golden beam of the torchlight stabbed through the darkness. It showed me a narrow passage, walled and roofed with huge stone slabs. Ahead lay a second opening, and once again I caught a whiff of cool damp air issuing from within. There was insufficient room to stand, and I was forced to crawl through into the chamber beyond.

Chapter Two
Gortnasheen

"We are the Sidhe."

In order for you to understand what happened next, what I saw and felt, I have to take a moment to say something about what I expected from such a place as this. Over a good part of Western Europe there are a large number of ancient megalithic sites. These date from Stone Age to Iron Age, that is, anything from around 4500 BC to 1500 BC and both earlier and later. They include the great stone circles or "henges" like Avebury and Stonehenge in Berkshire, or Brodgar in the Orkneys and Callanish in the Hebrides. In addition, there are the great hill figures like the Long Man of Wilmington in Sussex or the White Horse carved out of the chalk of the Marlborough Downs. There are also numberless grave sites, many dating from ancient times but reused in later ages—some for actual burial, others for ritual purposes. Thus, sites such as Waylands Smithy in Wiltshire, or the justly famous Newgrange in Ireland, despite being extensively excavated and written about, remain as mysterious to us today as they perhaps always were.

Many of these places stand as silent testimony to astonishing feats of engineering, the moving of vast stones and the unerring accuracy with which they were sited. Often the sheer size and impenetrability of the mindset that built them makes them seem daunting. And, of course, they have prompted an equally bewildering number of theories that attempt to "explain" their use and function. Everything from landing markers for alien space craft to complex astronomical observatories have been put forward over the past few years, and though some of these ideas have found partial acceptance among the academic community, most have not. In effect, we know as little about the real uses of these vast monuments as we do about the workings of the large percentage of our brains that appear never to be used at all.

This, then, was the background I had in my mind as I entered the site at Gortnasheen. Keith would probably have termed it a "passage grave" and we could both have listed at least a hundred of these scattered throughout Ireland and Scotland. Some had been discovered virtually intact—many still with the bodies of those who had been interred there, together with their often elaborate grave goods. Others—the most mysterious—contained elaborate carvings on their inner walls: elaborate spiraling patterns, zigzags, triangles and circles —the exact meaning of which remained uncertain—though the obvious significance to the people who carved them was widely acknowledged.

This gives an idea of what I was expecting: a stone chamber of maybe six to eight feet long and two or three feet wide, perhaps a carving or two, maybe (depending on the stage of Keith's work) a few scattered bones.

I pushed myself forward down the narrow passage, half crawling, half stooping, until I found the floor sloping away. At the same time the ceiling rose sharply, until I was able to stand up. I swung the torch around and had my first surprise of the day. The chamber must have measured some ten feet in length, and the roof was at least seven feet above me, allowing for the decline in the floor, which placed half the structure below ground level. Then, as I flashed the torch round, I had my second surprise—one of such magnitude that I gasped aloud.

I have mentioned that there were often carvings found on the walls within such sites, but these are normally numbered in dozens. Here, wherever I looked, there were carvings covering the walls in a riot of spiraling, twisting designs, some interlinked, others standing alone.

I must confess that I felt more than a little weak at the knees at that moment, and sat down rather more quickly than I had intended on the packed earth floor. From this vantage point I saw that the carvings continued right up into the roof where a corbelled dome, as fine as any piece of church architecture undertaken several millennia after this one had been created.

Then, as I swung the torch, my attention was drawn to a single glyph, larger than the rest, which dominated the eastern end of the chamber. For a moment I thought it actually glowed, and then realized that it must have been lined with crystals, which caught and threw back the light. (This was true. Later examination showed that hundreds of tiny rock crystals had been embedded in the rock to emphasize the importance of the carving.)

As I stared at the carving I felt again that strange prickling sensation—this time as strongly as I have ever felt it. My vision seemed to blur for a moment, and it seemed as though the image carved on the stone wavered. Then everything jumped back into focus. I was still sitting on the floor of the chamber, and glancing at my watch showed that only a few seconds had elapsed—yet in that time I felt as though I had been somewhere else for a lot longer. Just where that "somewhere else" might be I could not have said, but the feeling remained nonetheless.

I got up slowly and went across to examine the carving more closely. Slowly, I traced it with my fingers like someone reading braille. It was not an especially complex shape, a spiral of five coils with a perpendicular line extending from the uppermost outer edge through the centre and down below it. It seemed somehow familiar, and as I discovered later, it was one of several such glyphs that have been discovered at ancient sites in Ireland, Britain and (curiously) in the United States.

I stood there for a few moments more, trying to assemble my scattered thoughts and pin down exactly what it was that had made me feel strange a moment before. But, try as I might, I could not recapture the feeling, and it was also borne in upon me that Keith was waiting outside to hear my reaction.

Not without some reluctance, I crouched down and once again shuffled through the passageway. Outside the light seemed bright, though the day remained overcast. I found Keith hovering expectantly, his face an open question.

"You're right," I said. "It's astonishing, unique even. I've seen almost nothing as fine as this for years."

His face lit up at once and he began to talk faster than I had ever heard him. I don't remember exactly what it was he said — details of the discovery by a local man, his own excitement when he broke through the entrance and found what lay within, telling me that I must see the plans he had already made of the site.

We made our way back to his car and drove the few miles back to Dungarrow. I think I was mostly silent as we went, and no matter how I tried, I could not forget what I had seen, especially the larger spiral carving that had glowed back at me as though lit with its own fire.

I remember looking through Keith's detailed drawings, making all the right noises, asking all the right questions. But, in reality, I wanted to be on my own, to consider what I had seen without interruption. Finally, I detached myself from Keith on the excuse of needing to make some notes for the article he had invited me there to write. I made my way up to my room and closed the door with a sigh of relief. I took out my laptop and sat down at the rather rickety table by the window. But, though I sat there for an hour or more as the light slowly dimmed towards evening, I wrote no more than two or three sentences. My mind was elsewhere, thinking of everything I had ever read about sites of the kind I had just visited and especially of ancient glyphs like the one that had so deeply affected me.

Eventually I went to bed, though I could not sleep at first, lying for what seemed ages in the darkness, staring at the ceiling. Eventually I did drift off, and it was some time after this that I had one of the most powerful and disturbing dreams of my life. Reading it back now, it seems bizarre, and I will not be at all surprised if most of the people who read this account will think the author mad. And yet the dream, strange though it was, is nothing to what was to follow.

I dreamed that I was back under the mound of Gortnasheen, which seemed as if lit by flickering candlelight. I stood before the glyph, which glowed as though lit from within, unable to tear my eyes from its shape. Then slowly I became aware of a figure, standing off to one side. At first it was only dim and shadowy, but slowly it took on a more solid appearance—as a tall man dressed in archaic clothing of brown and green. He had long hair bound loosely with a circlet of silver. He had fine, delicate features that would have seemed feminine but for the strength of the jaw and the intense black eyes that stared back at me from beneath arched brows. It was, by any terms, one of the most beautiful faces I had ever seen.

"Who are you?" I heard myself ask.

"My name is of no importance," he replied. "I have come to you as a representative of my people."

"Who are your people?"

"We are the Sidhe." [pronounced Shee]

"The Sidhe?"

"An ancient race of this land. It is many hundreds of years since I walked above the earth."

"Why have you come?" I asked.

"Because the time is right. Because I have things to say that should be heard by your people. Before it is too late."

"I don't understand," I said.

"You will," he replied. "Go to the chamber again. Look at the carving. I shall come to you there."

Then he was gone, and in the same moment I woke, sitting up in

13

bed and staring at the fading pattern of the glyph that seemed to have burned itself into my mind.

I turned on the bedside light and looked at the clock. It was barely half past three and I had been asleep no more than two hours. The dream seemed so real that I could not get it out of my head. Finally, I took out my notebook and wrote down everything I could remember. The last words of my strange visitor, his injunction to go to the chamber and look at the carving again, made me uneasy, though I could not say why. In particular, the name he had spoken, the Sidhe, as being the race he represented, seemed familiar, though I could not remember exactly where I had heard it before.

The whole episode seemed crazy. Indeed, looking at what I have written here, it still seems so. Yet everything that followed stems from this, from my first visit to Gortnasheen and the dream that night. The battered old notebook is in front of me now, with the description of the dream written in rather shaky handwriting. I still question it, as often as I question all that followed; but the need to write it is stronger, and the message seems as imperative to me now as when I first heard it.

I lay down again and after a while drifted off into a sound and dreamless sleep. In the morning I reread what I had written and tried to dismiss the whole thing. But the truth was, taken together with the feelings I had experienced from the moment Keith Harris had phoned me, the visit to the mound at Gortnasheen, and then the dream, it all seemed somehow connected. In fact, the more I thought about the whole thing, the more certain I became that there was something in all this that I needed to fathom.

I washed and dressed and went downstairs in search of breakfast. I found Keith already ensconced over a plate of bacon, eggs and tomato and after ordering the same, exchanged a few pleasantries. Finally, having exhausted the topic of the weather, we fell silent for a while. At last, Keith could stand it no longer. "Well?" he said, "What do you think?"

"It's certainly a very interesting site," I said cautiously.

"And....?"

"Well, I'm going to need to do a bit of reading and research before I can write about it."

"But you will write something?" He seemed oddly disappointed, as though expecting me to say something else."

14

"I think so. Tell me..." I added, for the sake of something to say, "Do you happen to know what the name of the site means?"

"Gortnasheen? Well, a fair translation would be *Place of the Fairies*.

"The fairies?"

"Yes. You know, not those little tinselly-winged folk you read about in children's books—the real fairy race, the descendants of the Celtic gods. The Sidhe."

The word went through me like a hot knife, followed by a flood of images and thoughts. How could I have forgotten! I had read enough volumes of Celtic folklore and legend to know that Ireland was full of stories of the fairy people, who were nothing like the usual images invoked by the name. These fairies were tall and bright and powerful—very like gods indeed—and the old Gaelic name for them was Sidhe. They were a far cry from the mischievous dancers in circles beloved of the Victorians. No Tinkerbells these folk, with their powerful magic and unforgettable beauty and nobility. I remembered they were said to wear shoes of bronze, and to possess vast treasure-houses stuffed with gold and jewels. Sometimes wandering people would accidentally stumble into one of their houses, which looked like mounds of earth on the outside but were huge and full of wonders within. And time stretched and slipped for such visitors, so that when they returned hundreds of years had passed, though to them it seemed only a few.

Suddenly my dream made sense—or at least, a kind of crazy sense.

My mouth must have been hanging open for a while, or maybe my silence worried him, because Keith interrupted the flow of thoughts by asking me if I was OK.

"Oh. Yes, "I said, "Just thinking." I made an effort to focus. "I'd like to go and take another look at the site. Maybe spend a bit of time there on my own. If that's OK?"

"Of course," Keith said. He seemed relieved. "I have to go into Dublin this morning. Why don't I let you off at the site and pick you up later? You'll have at least a few hours."

So it was agreed, and I went to gather up my notebook. We drove in silence out to the site and Keith waved a cheery farewell before turning the car around and driving off in a cloud of exhaust fumes. I watched him go and turned to look at the mound. What on earth was I doing here? Then I remembered the dream, and my strange visitor's injunction to me to return to the place. Well, I had done so. What would happen next I had no idea, but I knew that I had to go inside the mound if I wanted to find out.

Crawling in through the narrow entranceway, I again found the torch set back in the niche. With it were two candles and a box of matches that I decided to take with me. Part of me, I now realize, was already determined to recreate the scene of my dream, right down to the flickering candlelight.

Once inside I lit both candles and set them on the ground on either side of the (as I found I now thought of it) Great Glyph. Then I turned off the torch and sat in front of it, feeling faintly ridiculous.

What happened next I am still unsure about, though in retrospect it is obvious enough. Perhaps I fell asleep. Perhaps I dreamed. But whatever the truth (and ultimately it remains unimportant), I found myself facing a shadowy figure that gradually became clearer until I looked again into the eyes of the figure from my dream. This time he seemed more solid somehow, as though my familiarity with his form gave it greater definition. I saw that his long hair had a silvery tinge to it — though his face was unlined. But to apportion an age in years to this being was and is meaningless. He was both old and young, ageless and timeless as all such messengers must be.

Neither then nor later did I feel any fear in his presence. This may seem strange, since most of us (myself included) are not used to talking with beings from another place. But from the first, the presence of my visitor and the dialogues I had with him seemed absolutely natural. I never once felt under any kind of threat. To the contrary, there was a great feeling of friendship and companionship that always issued from his presence. I make this response in answer to all who ask: how did you know you could trust this being? I simply knew, right from the start, that I could do so. It was a feeling that never went away.

"I am glad you have come," he said. His voice, I noticed, was light but resonant, as though he spoke from a place where there was a kind of echo.

"I need to know more," I answered. This seemed the best way to go about it.

A flash of a smile split his serious face. "That is what we hoped," he said.

"Who are you?" I asked.

"I am one of the Sidhe, those whom you call the fairy race."

"Are you real?"

"That all depends on what you mean by real."

"Can I touch you?"

"If it will make it easier for you to believe in me."

I reached out with my not altogether steady fingers and touched one slender hand where it rested at his waist. What did I feel? I still find it hard to relate. It was as though I touched something that was both present and not present, solid and yet not solid. His "flesh"—if flesh it was—seemed cool to the touch, and somehow insubstantial. Yet it was undoubtedly real, at least as I understood it. I saw what he meant by a consideration of "what I meant by real." This was something wholly new to me. I had no criteria by which to measure it.

I withdrew my hand, trying not to do so too quickly, struggling with my thoughts and impressions. When in doubt, I thought, ask a question.

"Why have you chosen to speak to me?"

"Because it is time to do so. Because you will listen. Because we have much to tell your race while you can still hear us."

"Not many people can these days," I said.

"That is true, and it makes what we have to tell you all the more urgent."

"What shall I call you?" I asked.

"Names are too powerful to be given so easily. I would not call you by your name, yet we are speaking, are we not?"

I nodded.

"Very well then, let us just say that I am of the Sidhe and you are of the human kind. That is sufficient to enable us to talk, is it not?"

"Of course", I said. "But—how shall we do this?"

"I suggest that I speak and you listen," replied my visitor, with a hint of a smile.

"May I take notes?"

"If you so desire."

And so he began what was to be the first of many conversations—or perhaps monologues would be a better word, since I seldom spoke except to ask for clarifying questions. I seldom wrote down anything as I was too caught up in the words and thoughts that issued from the lips of my communicator. I simply forgot, entranced by the message from one world to another.

But I seldom forgot what he said, and indeed found it easy to recall everything with a sharpness of memory that was quite foreign to me. Nor did it seem appropriate to record any of his words electronically. Indeed, I once tried to do so but without success. Though I murmured his words into the microphone somewhat like a translator, the tape that emerged was blank.

At the end of that first encounter within the mound, I asked if we would continue our discussions, and if so, how. I knew that I could not always return to the site, the future of which was, as with all such excavations, uncertain. By way of answer my visitor from the Sidhe told me to take a tracing of the Glyph, and later to make a fair copy. Once I had done this, I need only fix it to a wall and sit before it in contemplation and he would be able to make contact with me. When it came to the writing of this book, and the possibility of its publication, I was for a time uncertain about reproducing the Glyph. But my communicator assured me that the more who saw it, the more there would be who might experience for themselves the power of the Sidhe. To this end I have included brief instructions at the end of this book to assist those who might feel moved to do so, to enter this strange and wonderful dialogue for themselves.

In the weeks that followed I was in almost daily contact with the representative of the Sidhe. What follows is a record, largely from accounts written at high speed at the end of each conversation, beginning with that first time at Gortnasheen. I believe them to be largely accurate, though I may occasionally have used words that my visitor did not. In any case I am certain that the essence of what is recorded here reflects as closely as possible the things that were said or meant. Occasionally there is a certain amount of repetition, as there will be in any conversation, as topics are diverged from and then returned to. I have resisted the temptation to tidy these up, preferring to allow the patterns of the ongoing dialogue to come through as I heard it.

What emerged still seems to me astonishing. It is my hope that others may find it as enlightening and inspiring as I have, even though they may never have the grace to hear the measured words of the Sidhe from the lips of one of their race.

Chapter Three

Beginnings

"You must seek to become reconnected to everything."

At the beginning of that first conversation in the mound of Gortnasheen I had more questions to ask of my visitor from the Sidhe than at any other. How could I understand my communicator, since he must certainly have spoken a language that was no longer widely accessible and which I myself certainly did not understand? Could others see him? Where did he come from? Other similar questions came to mind.

Some of these questions he turned aside politely with a shrug or a few words only, until I learned that it was better to listen than to question. He did, however, tell me that others could not, in general, see him—at least unless he chose for them to do so, and that was a rare event. I could understand him likewise because he wanted me to: whatever language he actually spoke I heard it in everyday English. As to his place of origin, I understood that was to be described later. To begin with he wanted to tell me about his own people, the Sidhe, and why they had chosen this moment to speak through me.

So, let me begin, as my visitor began, on the 11th July, 1998, sometime around 11:00 a.m. within the mound of Gortnasheen.

"We are an ancient people. We were here long before your kind walked on this earth. We remember everything and have seen everything that took place here for many thousands of your years. We ourselves do not measure time as you do, so that for us time passes slowly. We do not speak of our origins to anyone not of our race; but it is certain that we emerged from the earth as you yourselves did, though much sooner in the history of the world.

"For a long time we were alone, save for the creatures who shared the world with us. In that time we lived above the earth, under the sun and moon and stars, which we loved to look upon. We dreamed and sang and told stories of the first days. We seldom mated and even less often gave birth, for we were and are a long-lived people and our numbers remained constant for many hundreds of your years.

"Then one day we became aware of the Newcomers, strange people who lived mostly in caves or holes scraped from the earth. They were large and slow of movement and wit, and, as we swiftly learned, could be both savage and cruel. They hunted the great creatures with whom we shared the land, and on one occasion they hunted us—bringing the first death to our people in many ages.

"At first our leaders were of a mind to drive them out, even to kill them (yes, we knew then, as now, how to ape the ways of your race, even to the stage of killing). But others spoke of moving from the places where these Newcomers dwelled into places where they would not come. And of erecting barriers they might not cross. This policy won, and so we began a pattern of hiding that has become second nature to us. Few of your race have seen us since that time, though we have continued to live side by side with humankind. We have watched you grow and seen that you have changed very little since the time of the Newcomers. Still you love to kill and drive each other out of places you believe to be yours. You have destroyed many places and many species have been driven to extinction or to its verge. And so we have hidden ourselves ever deeper and further away from you.

"To begin with we lived in the wildest places, far from the territory of the Newcomers. But gradually they hunted further and further and we were forced to withdraw ever deeper into the land. At last we went below the earth, making caverns for ourselves, lit by strange suns and moons. We became to you the People of the Hollow Hills, the Dwellers Beneath the Mounds, the Fairy People, the Little Dark Ones, as you called us. But always we were the Sidhe.

"So seldom were we seen that we became part of your mythology. Things that you did not understand or could not fully see you banished to the dark corners of your minds, calling us bogies or bogeymen, making us into fearful things to frighten naughty children. But all the time we watched, we changed but little, and always we waited for a sign that you might change also, that you might be willing to see us, to speak with us.

"Some there have been, in recent years as you measure time, who have recognized us and honored our difference. Some have told the truth about us and have been labeled madmen, their words too fantastic to be real, by your wise men and women. Those who spoke of our existence have been laughed at and made to feel foolish, so that they fell silent. You should know that this will happen to you also. But, there are some who will listen, some who will hear what we have to say. Thus I have chosen to speak with you, believing that you will listen and that others will listen to you. Record all that I have to say and let others read it. Perhaps there will be time to change the course of your history and avert the disaster that is coming upon you."

At this point I tried to find out what exactly this disaster might be, but my companion would speak of it no more at that time. I must confess that having read all too often such predictions from beings outside the normal sphere of life, I was doubtful, but my companion dismissed my doubts.

"I do not say these things in order to frighten you into belief. The world will go on anyway. The question is whether it does so with or without your kind. There are those among us who believe you should be allowed to perish, but others, myself among them, believe otherwise. We believe that a new era may be about to dawn, in which the people of the Sidhe will come forth again and be seen by all. If that is to happen, you must be prepared for it, and thus I speak to you of our history and the message we would bring to you all. I would speak no more of these things now, but we shall have more to say of them in the time to come."

At this point my companion fell silent and I began to question him as to how our conversations were to continue. When he had explained how this was to be, he took his leave of me abruptly, fading back into the walls of the chamber. I sat for a long while after this, wondering if I had really gone mad, if anything I had heard was true or not. I was to wonder this many times in the days that followed. I have always had a healthy distrust of what might be termed "channeled" literature; yet here I was receiving material that was clearly intended to be shared among others.

Living at the beginning of the twenty-first century I have seen an increase in this type of writing, and so much of it sounds the same knell of doom for mankind which my naturally optimistic view finds hard to accept. Indeed, I was several times to question my communicator regarding the somewhat negative accent which some of his words had. And yet I continued to "tune in" to my companion from the Sidhe, to listen and record all that he had to say.

Why did I do this? Ultimately, I believe, because I felt that the nature of what was being presented had a quality to it that was outside anything I had come across before. If, as some will doubtless think, I was simply talking with a subpersonality, some part of my own psyche, then all I can say is that I wish I could always access that part of me, since it seems so much wiser and more knowledgeable than my usual self!

As time passed I became as familiar with his presence as I would with any flesh and blood person, though I never ceased to be aware that he was of another order. Also, I read everything I could find about the fairy folk and their history, finding details that confirmed what my communicator had told me. Eventually, I ceased to question the veracity of his words and simply listened, advice that I offer to all who read this. (See "Further Reading," pp. 111)

Just how important it is to believe the origin of these words I cannot say. The words themselves, and the ideas expressed, are what matter. I have become convinced that our future development, even our survival as a species, may depend upon this. Words I know that will seem presumptuous or even deranged. For myself, I can only offer the words of the Sidhe for all to read who wish to. Whether you choose to believe or disbelieve is a matter for your own heart and mind.

Later on the same day that I had my first conversation with the Sidhe, Keith returned from Dublin to pick me up. I said nothing of what had occurred and it seemed that, having introduced me to the site, his part in the matter had come to an end. There were no more veiled references to "something unusual" about Gortnasheen, and the air of slight unease or embarrassment that I had detected earlier seemed to have vanished. I became convinced that the Sidhe had in some way influenced him, and that it was this that resulted in his calling upon me to visit the site before the more august journalists who would soon be reporting on the discovery. In another way, perhaps, he also sought a kind of confirmation of his own half-understood feelings about the site.

That evening I was on a plane home. Once back in London I

settled down to write a perfectly straightforward account of the site and its wondrous carvings. The whole episode at Gortnasheen might have seemed like a dream, save for the enlarged image of the Glyph that was pinned up in my study, where I could see it every day. That, and of course the communications that flowed from the representative of the Sidhe.

Almost daily during the next few weeks (an astonishingly short time considering all that I received) whenever other commitments allowed, I would draw the curtains and, having lit a candle on either side of the image, sit down before the Glyph. There my communicator would appear, dimly at first, but with ever strengthening power, until I could see him standing before me. Then, we would converse, and afterwards I would write down an account of our conversation. It is these conversations that form the content of the chapters that follow, and that I have reproduced here with the minimum of comment. That the experience changed me is beyond question, and I have occasionally included something of what happened to me in the world while I was receiving the communications. I do this not to make any special claims, but merely to offer some kind of measure against which those who follow the text and the ideas expressed here can decide for themselves.

My second conversation with the being of the Sidhe took place at my home in Oxford. I had wondered if in fact I would be able to receive anything, as we were not only no longer in the sacred chamber, but away from the soil of Ireland, but I need not have worried. Apparently the image of the Glyph was sufficient to form the link necessary, and my visitor was present within minutes of my beginning to concentrate on it.

I began with a question. "You spoke of having observed us from a very distant time. Can you say more about that?"

"Indeed. For it is in part because of what we have seen that we have chosen to speak with you at this time. You are about to enter a new era, to cross a barrier of time that you have called the Millennium. You look at this artificial moment as a symbol of new hope—as though the mere counting of divisions of time could bring about a change. In reality, you are indeed upon the edge of a new beginning, a new age in which you will develop and change in ways that you cannot begin to understand. But it is not of these things that I would speak, but rather

26

of the preparations that you can make before such changes may be experienced.

"I speak of a new integration of things that you have long since broken into small parts. Just as you have isolated yourselves from the world around you, so you have isolated yourself from your own inner selves. Your spirit and heart and mind are separate within you, some not even acknowledged. You must bring these severed parts together again if you are to prepare yourselves for the coming changes. As long as you continue to act as if you had a warring tribe within you, you cannot be whole. Yet wholeness is what you must aim for, otherwise you will continue to fragment until there is nothing left but broken crumbs of your true selves.

"In the beginning it was not always thus. Though when the Newcomers arrived they were slow and brutal, yet they understood that they were part of everything, that every action they performed in one place had an effect in another. Thus the harmony of creation was stable; every living thing was part of this balance, and while each played its part that balance remained.

"But soon, though it was much later as you reckon time, things changed. You changed. You began to forget that you were part of the whole. Instead you saw yourselves as a dominant species. From there it was but a short space to believing yourselves lords of the earth, with dominion over others, especially the animals whom you now began to destroy in greater and greater numbers. Even the Newcomers had known that they need take only what they needed—for clothing, for food, and for shelter.

"You in your newfound power began to take more because it was there to take. You sought to build great stocks of everything, judging this as wealth. Soon you began to take from the earth also, stealing the bright hidden tokens you call jewels, or the rich yellow blood you call gold—always in the belief that the possession of such things made you even more powerful.

"In fact that power was short-lived, and it has remained so to this day. Yet the Earth has been ravaged without cease, until it is almost bereft of its richest possessions. Even the very life-blood of

27

the world—that which you call uranium—has been taken out and its true function twisted to create weapons."

All of this was delivered without passion, though it might have been seen as an indictment of humankind. At this point I asked a question about the true purpose of uranium, and my companion answered as follows:

"The true use of this earth-blood is to keep the temperature and energy of the Earth constant. By taking so much of it from within the world, this has become unbalanced. This is something that will require dealing with in time to come. It is all part of the way that your species have fallen out of alignment with the rest of your world. By placing yourselves at the summit of creation, you have lost sight of your true status.

"That, as I have said, is as an equal part of the web of all things. You would be better to see yourselves as allies of creation rather than its rulers. By choosing to work in harmony with the natural world—as once all living things did—you could still redress the balance.

"If your life brushes against that of another creature, you feel something. If you take the life of another creature, you feel something. It is no great step to extend this to feeling something when you touch a rock or a tree, when you feel the energy of a river or the sea.

"Many feel these things, yet your race continually shut out these feelings. Just as you attach devices to your horses so that they can see only ahead, so you have done to yourselves, limiting your vision until you can see nothing save that which is before you. Only when you learn to remove the guards will you experience true vision. You must seek to become reconnected to everything and to end the separation you have created for yourselves."

Thoroughly intrigued by this, I asked how we might achieve such a thing.

"The answer is too complex to give in a single moment. There are many things you can do to bring about a reconnection. Begin by noticing the world around you. By truly looking. By seeing past the surface of things to the level of Spirit.

"At the moment when you go out into nature you see only the surface of things. Trees, grass, water, plants. Yet the reality of these things is far greater. Once you knew this. You can discover it again if you truly wish. Next time you are outside look around you. Try to see beyond the surface into the true nature of the things you see. Though you may find it difficult to do so at first, in time you will begin to see more and more. If you continue far enough and deeply enough you will even begin to communicate with the spirit within the things you are observing. In truth you will cease to be observers at all and become part of the thing you are looking at.

"This is what the ancient bards of this land meant when they spoke of having "been" a thing. This was more than a poetic image, but a very real truth. To truly know a thing is to become one with it. Just as to become one with it is to truly know it.

"When you do this you will begin to understand the true nature of things and your own relationship to them. Perhaps then, when plants and rocks and animals are no longer soulless things, you will cease to treat them as such, cease to take them and use them as you have now for so many of your ages. If you are truly ready to enter a new era then you must discover how to make such changes to the way you view things. Only when you have done so will you be truly liberated from the narrow place in which you have put yourselves.

"At present you are just as much prisoners as if you were truly locked up within stone walls. The walls of your prison are not ones that you can see with your eyes, but they can still be recognized. Once you have done that you can begin to deal with the walls in your own time. But this will only begin to happen when you have taken the first steps towards acknowledging the reality of your relationship to everything. Once that has happened then other realizations will follow. Remember, you are part of the divine whole. Only when you recognize this will you begin to move forward, and to become what you are destined to be."

At this point I began to grow tired. Although during the weeks that followed I became used to the strange experience of listening to my visitor, it never wholly ceased to have this effect. The effort of attending to, and then of recording, the messages that came to me in this way took more energy than I realized.

I have read since that others who have experienced this type of communication have found fatiguing the effort of keeping the line of communication open. At any rate, this concluded the first day of my dialogue with the Sidhe.

At the end I felt bewildered, disbelieving even. After all I had felt and experienced I was still aware that I had been sitting in my room, staring at a drawing that somehow enabled me to both see and hear a being who was neither of my own race nor kind, and who was not, indeed, visible to anyone else. On the face of it, the whole thing was ridiculous, and I came as near in that moment as I ever did thereafter to abandoning the whole thing.

With hindsight, I am glad I did not. The experience of talking with the Sidhe changed me in all kinds of ways—I think for the better. It certainly opened my eyes to things that I might never otherwise have considered. It is my hope that the same thing will be true for those who read this account, even if you never put into practice any of the teachings offered here.

Chapter Four

Reunion

"Spirit is that which animates everything."

The next day I was awake early and sat before the image of the Great Glyph. Almost at once my visitor appeared before me, seeming as solid and real as anyone I might meet in the street—though certainly very different to look at! I began by asking what he had meant by the "fragmentation of the self." His answer was swift and detailed.

"Once every part of your being was whole, each part related to the other, head to heart, heart to hand, hand to mind, mind to soul. But, as time passed, you have separated these things, these aspects of yourselves, into many small packages. Many now do not even acknowledge the presence of Spirit within everything, even within your own selves. Despite the evidence that is daily given to you, you still turn away from such things as trivial or of little use. Yet, the gift of Spirit is a great one, for it not only connects you to everything else, it connects you to yourself.

"How many of your kind are weary and listless? How many feel that they are spending their time fruitlessly and without reason? We see many thousands who daily give away the gift of life in order to acquire more and more possessions, without any real understanding of why they do so. They have become like machines, enacting the same movements every day without understanding or feeling. This is due in part to the loss of Spirit, this state of un-connectedness that you have created for yourselves."

I pointed out here that for many people spirit had a religious connotation that they could not accept.

"Acknowledging the presence of Spirit does not require the kind of belief you are referring to. To those like ourselves who have been here longer than man, your systems of belief are all as one. Many of the teachers you most revere have spoken of these things, but they can still be seen as existing outside specific doctrines.

"Spirit is that which animates everything. When you see a fly, or a fish, or a bird, it has life. If you choose to see life as a series of reflexes, then of course you will not be able to perceive the actions of

34

Spirit in all things. Yet it is just this presence that tells us that a thing has life. It is not the ability to think, or even to create, those actions by which you set so great a store that defines what is alive.

"The humblest creature contributes to the whole, though it may never speak, or form a thought, or create anything other than more of its own kind. It has life. It possesses Spirit. In this it is no different from any one of your kind, or from any stone or tree or river. All possess life, and all possess Spirit. Life is Spirit, and Spirit is life. Surely this is simple enough to understand!"

A good deal of what my visitor had just said was familiar to me in one form or another from my readings. I knew there was an essential problem for many people who heard such things. I said: "Many are not able to see what you call Spirit."

"Only because they have cut themselves off from an understanding of what it means to be alive. You have become too concerned with the process of what you see as life. You live for a few brief years and then you are gone. If you consider what you were before or what you will be afterwards, it is only to consider whether your lot will be one of comfort or punishment.

"Even those who speak of enlightenment, who try to transcend the concern of all humanity with the things of the flesh, still concern themselves with ideas of perfection. Our experience of these things is that there is no such thing as perfection. We continue to evolve. Even the Sidhe, who grow so slowly compared to humankind, even we do this. In the last thousand years we have changed little, but before that we underwent a number of changes that made us very different from what we were before."

When I asked for more details of this my visitor shrugged his shoulders.

"It is not as you would understand. The changes to which I refer are not definable in your speech. They are not improvements or developments, but rather changes in the way we relate to creation.

"We have found that the veils between the worlds have grown thinner with time, and as they have changed so has our sense of awareness of the realms that are beyond our normal senses. In time we believe this will happen to you also, but maybe not for many hundreds of your years. We will watch this with interest, just as we shall watch to see if you survive."

"How can we help ourselves to develop in this way?" I asked then.

"There are many ways to do this. Simply by paying attention you will learn more than you can by studying the details of the dimension in which you find yourselves. You can learn much in this way, but far more can be achieved by stillness and attentiveness to everything. By recognizing its relationship to everything else as I have said.

"As long as you continue to separate everything into small parts, you will understand less and less. As individuals, I would say that you should practice observing the true nature of everything. Do this by sitting still and banishing the many thoughts that fill your minds and distract you from truly seeing and feeling. That way you will learn to reconnect. Once you are reconnected you will begin to perceive the patterns within the whole."

"And this will help us to restore our own inner unity?"

"Yes. As you begin to glimpse the unity within everything, so you will begin to perceive the unity you once had but have since lost. The unity of spirit and mind, heart and head, soul and body that will lead the way to deeper awareness of what you can be.

"First must come a recognition of Spirit, for from this flows much else. Spirit is the centre around which all else revolves. It sends forth messages that are heard by the rest, and so gradually the disharmony which is the soul-note of your being at this time will become harmonized again. You will feel once more part of the great whole and become aware of much that has been lost to you through the ages.

"It may even be that you will be able to perceive us clearly without need of such devices as the Glyph. That remains to be seen, for there is a great deal of suspicion of those that are other than yourselves.

"Now, I sense you are growing tired. Let us continue at another time."

My visitor withdrew at once, leaving me with a sense of rising excitement. If only a quarter of what he was saying was true, then humanity as a species was about to enter the most exciting—and challenging—age it had ever experienced! Despite my tiredness I could not wait for the next session.

In fact it was to be several days before I got back to my study and to the Great Glyph. Work took me elsewhere, but in all that time I never ceased to think about the experience I was undergoing, and to wonder at its meaning.

When I was finally able to continue my dialogue with the Sidhe, I asked again about the need for reunification of the scattered being of humanity. My visitor had this to say of the causes behind our failure to be satisfied by anything:

"There never before has been a time when you have had the opportunity to follow whatever calls out to you. Yet it seems that your lives are disappointing and dull. You are ever determined to seek some new enterprise or diversion to raise your spirits. Entertainment has become a god to you, the most important thing in your lives—yet you are still dissatisfied at heart.

"This emptiness at the centre of your being is something that will only be answered by reestablishing the unity of Spirit that places you once again near the heart of creation.

"At present the restlessness and dissatisfaction you feel are fueled by a belief that your lives are without deeper meaning. So you bemoan your lot and express your dissatisfaction by longing for ever more complex adjuncts to living.

"Often your dissatisfaction with life is expressed as anger, and anger itself takes shape and form when it is so often uttered. We see anger walking everywhere in your world, given shape and form by its constant renewal. If you could learn to give as much attention and energy to less negative aspects of your life, you would see immediate improvement in the way you feel.

"Fragmentation of the spirit is at the heart of these feelings you experience. Because you are no longer in touch with the many aspects of yourself, the world around you has lost the freshness it once had.

"The links between heart and mind, body and spirit are deeply broken in many of your kind. If you could only learn to reunite these links, reestablish contact with your own sundered selves, the world in which you live would once again shine forth in all its old beauty."

I asked at once how we might do this.

"Many things of which I have already spoken are important here. Inner stillness, greater attention to everything around you—and within you. A sense of communion with the natural world and the ancient harmony of your selves. These are all a part of the way in which primal harmony can be restored.

"You are used to thinking back to a period of great disharmony, of chaos, from which you believe all life emerged; but already there are those among you—scientists and thinkers—who are beginning to recognize the essential unity of all things. Once this is understood by more of your kind, a change will take place and you will begin to feel reconnected to the universe and to each other and to both the visible and invisible worlds around you. This will bring greater balance and a real sense of life that will banish the grayness and dullness you feel.

"We never lost sight of this deep harmony of all living things, which are linked by the presence of Spirit in whatever way that may manifest. These things of which I speak are given to you in order that you may once again become aware of the true unity of all things—of yourselves and the worlds around you, of things both seen with your eyes and things seen by your spirit.

"What more clear indication of the way you have relegated spiritual matters to a level of disbelief or scorn than the response received by many of your greatest visionaries in recent times. Even now, when the world around you teems with energy and when more and more of your race are enabled to see these things with the eyes of the Spirit, there is constant mockery of such things.

"Be aware that you, too, will receive such a response if you choose to share these words with others. But if only a few listen and understand what we are saying, that will have justified this communication. Whether this will be enough to bring about the change we hope to see is another matter. But we are hopeful."

As I listened to this I became increasingly uncomfortable. While I recognized the truth of what I was hearing, another aspect became more and more pressing. As a father myself, I had become alarmed at the direction in which I saw the young headed—towards what I could only see as a time of greater and greater destructiveness. I wondered what the Sidhe might have to say of this and what—if anything—we should be saying to our children.

My communicant was silent for several moments after I asked this. When he spoke again I seemed to detect certain unease in his tone of voice—the only time I felt this in our conversations.

"This is not an easy thing for us to answer. We reproduce only rarely and therefore do not encounter the problem of which you speak. Yet I will say this: you are right to feel concern for the future of your children, for there is indeed a negativity and destructiveness about them that is very powerful. In part this is because you have failed to instruct them in the matters of Spirit, or to encourage the needful respect for all living things.

"I am aware this is no easy thing, but it is important to show your young that there is a greater mystery than they know of at the heart of the universe. This is something that goes far deeper than the ancient issues of generation, which we know has always plagued you. Nor is it sufficient to speak to them of the beliefs you possess, for the truths they seek are deeper than any system of which you are aware.

"There is a very real danger that many of the rising generation will bring such a negative energy to their lives that a break in the chain of being may occur. If they are unaware, or disbelieve the presence of Spirit, then how are their children to learn of these things? In two generations all respect for the deeper matters of life could be expunged. After this, there will be little chance for you to find the path to wholeness again.

"As to what you may say to your children now, I believe that this can only be a question of showing by example. If they see only the dark, destructive side of your natures now, how are they to understand there is anything else? Yet despite these things I have said, there is still hope. There are many among your young who perceive us (not only the very young) and are aware of the greater meaning of the world.

"I cannot say whether there are enough of them to turn the tide, but I do believe that if your race is to make the return to harmony possible they must do so at least in part by showing the young the true nature of life. It may well be in the nature of your kind that many will not hear what you say, but you must at least try.

"Beyond this, the best you can do is to offer unconditional love to your children, and do not expect more from them than they can give. These things may seem overly clear to you, but there are many who do not recognize the need for such things. Speak, then, openly of these matters. Do not seek to impose your ideas, but rather to offer them as gifts to your children. Perhaps enough will listen and understand to turn the tide."

At this point I felt the conversation had come to an end, but before the link was broken my companion continued.

"There is another matter, not unconnected to this question that I would speak of. This concerns the importance of the ancestors in your lives and in your future. This may seem surprising to you, since

40

for your kind the ancestors are in the past and have no influence on your lives beyond that of recollection and memory.

"Yet the ancient people of these lands believed that the influence of the ancestors became stronger as time passed, and this is true now also. By ancestors I do not simply mean the fathers and mothers, or the grandparents of each individual. Rather I refer to the ancient wise ones who hold the memory of your race and kind, and much wisdom besides.

"Think of it thus: that there is a great storehouse of ancestral knowledge that is available for you to access whenever it is needed. Much that I have told you is already known to your ancestors and could have been accessed at any time in the past ages. Not all the ancestors have known incarnation as you would understand it; rather they are present in the Otherworld as nodes of energy around which have grown a shell of wisdom and understanding generated by your living spiritual being.

"If each and every one of your kind has learned something from the experience of incarnation then all of this knowledge has been stored in the essence of the ancestors. There is indeed much deep teaching regarding this subject, which I will speak of again, but for the moment let yourself become accustomed to the thought that there are those in the Otherworld to whom you have access simply by tuning in to the possibility of their presence.

"And, on the matter of your children, you might well place them in the care of their ancestral guardians."

"You mean, like guardian angels?" I asked.

"Indeed, that would be as close as you could come to understanding this mystery at the moment. If each child is possessed of a guardian from among the ancestors—and let me say again that this does not need to be one of their own bloodline—then they will become more open to an understanding of the presence of Spirit in all things, and will be protected to some extent from the destructiveness of the age into which they are born.

41

"For you also, whatever your age or generation, an understanding of the gifts offered to you by the ancestors is important. Think of them as channels for an ancient wisdom that transcends any specific belief or teaching. This is the most simple and yet the most profound wisdom of all. From them you may learn much, and like we of the Sidhe they are part of a continuing movement towards reunification of Spirit in all."

At the end of this conversation I felt an overwhelming urge to go out for a walk. My mind was full of the words of the Sidhe, and I wanted nothing more than to go out and share them with others. Yet, at this stage, I knew this was not an option. A few days into the experience, I was still filled with doubts and uncertainties. I thought again of the words of my visitor, of his instruction to observe more and more in order to silence the chattering thoughts that distract us so much as we go about our daily lives.

My steps turned in the direction of my local park, an oasis of green amongst the concrete and glass of Oxford. It was a favorite place of mine to go when I was working on a new book or article. Here I could resolve the ideas I was struggling to put into words. Nearly always I would come back energized, ready to sit down at my desk and work for several hours at a time.

As I walked I thought of what my communicator had said about the original sense of community that existed between humans and the natural world. I found myself looking at a particularly fine oak tree that had brought me and others hours of shade from the heat of the summer sun.

Today, I tried to see more deeply into the nature of this tree — and was rewarded by a sense that I was looking not just at something with trunk, branches and leaves, but something that possessed a spirit of its own. It's not easy to describe this. The tree remained a tree; yet it also became something more — a kind of link between two states of being, two aspects of the world, human and plant.

Drawn by this feeling, I lay down beneath the branches of the old oak, and, as I had done countless times before, stared up through the branches at the patches of blue sky that showed through. As I did so a sense of stillness and peace descended on me. The constant hum of traffic noise faded away, leaving me with a sense of deep contentment. I might have been anywhere in the world other than in the middle of a busy city.

Perhaps I fell asleep for a time. But I became aware of the presence of the representative of the Sidhe, not as a solid presence as when I sat before the Glyph, but like a wind-borne spirit drifting lazily through the park. No words were exchanged, yet it was as though a ripple of response went through the earth itself, and certainly through the tree. It seemed that some silent words had been spoken, which I could not hear, but to which the world around me responded with delight. Even more wondrous, I felt something in me respond also—not to the being from the Sidhe, but to the other realm that surrounded and interacted with mine. It was as though the growing things that were all around me— trees, grass, flowers in their carefully tended beds, suddenly became aware of me—and that I was listening, really looking, really sensing their own unique signature. And they were glad, very glad indeed, and sent back their own response by seeing me!

The sensation lasted maybe a moment only, and then I was back, aware again of people passing, of the steady rumble of traffic, of a jumbo jet passing over Oxford. But just for that moment I felt that my senses had been extended outward, further than ever before. If this was what the Sidhe meant by reconnecting with the web of creation, then I wanted to experience it again, even to make it a permanent part of my rapport with the world around me.

I walked home as full of wonder as when I had started, but now with a new sense of purpose. I would indeed listen to the Sidhe, and even if I was not always able to feel this certain of their truth, I would at least give them the benefit of the doubt and do my best to follow the wisdom they seemed so willing to share.

Chapter Five

Incarnation

"There are many ways in which the world where
we dwell and your world are the same."

My curiosity about my visitor grew stronger every day. By now I had read more about the Celtic fairy race; but I found most of the books either repetitive or vague. Some believed them to be no more than a memory of an older race—perhaps the Picts who once lived in the northern area of the island. Others—the majority it seemed—believed the fairy folk to be no more than a projection of the human mind—much like angels. Yet, here and there, I came across accounts like those collected by the great folklorist W.Y. Evans-Wentz in his 1911 book, *The Fairy Faith In Ireland*, which not only took the existence of the Sidhe seriously, but also described beings not unlike my own visitor.

It was about this time that I decided, after lot of soul-searching, to talk to an old friend about my experience. It was to be his prompting, as well as a desire to know more, that led me to take the bull by the horns and ask for more direct information about the Sidhe themselves.

David Spangler is a well known teacher and natural philosopher whose lively and enquiring mind has often acted as a sounding board for my wilder flights of fancy over the years. I felt that if anyone could give me an unbiased, clearheaded response to the communications I was receiving from the Sidhe, it was he.

I phoned him one evening, and after a brief exchange of news launched into a fairly detailed account of the events at Gortnasheen and all that had followed on from there. "Am I going crazy?" I asked when I had poured it all out.

"Not a bit," replied David. "This is fascinating. Can you send me the stuff you've been getting?"

I agreed to do so, and posted a fat package of notes to my friend. A few days later he called me.

"It's all extraordinary stuff all right. Reads pretty well too. I think it's on the level." He went on to express some doubts over the somewhat negative aspects of the opening communication, but ended by saying that he totally supported what I was doing and looked forward to reading more.

After this I sent regular bulletins of my continuing dialogues, receiving detailed and excited responses. After a while David began to supply me with questions that helped to broaden the approach to my communicator. Many of the most searching queries came from this source, and I am glad to acknowledge both the support and fellowship of my friend throughout the experience of the Sidhe communications.

My own curiosity about this mysterious race that had chosen to contact me began with a simple enough question: I wished to know more about them, about their nature and being. The response I received was so interesting that I spent several more days exploring the history of the Sidhe. My visitor's first response was guarded:

"These are not topics that are easy to discuss. We are not like you, despite the similarity in our outer appearance. As I said before we were both of the earth as you were, but at some point our lives diverged—you might say that we "evolved" differently. Not only is this the case, but also we entered at a different point in the creation of the universe and thus we exist in a parallel state that is also tangential to your understanding of the world.

"When I spoke of our dwelling under the earth, of making places to dwell, I did not mean that we dwelled there in an actual realm that was beneath the earth as you understand it. Rather, I would see it as existing both in the realm where we have our being, and in your realm at the same time. As though both places occupied the same space but were separated in some way.

"There are many ways in which the world where we dwell and your world are the same. In both there is relationship to each other that is intended to enable us to share the spirit of the world, to experience that which unites everything. Both your race and mine experience this, but differently. Thus we experience time in a different way, as I have already mentioned."

I found this hard to follow, and asked if he could define any of these ideas in a broader way.

"I will try. Time is an essence in which we are contained. It is as real as any substance and yet it has no substance, no form that we can recognize. I have already referred to the fact that your measurement of days and hours is purely artificial, and yet we also measure time, and recognize its nature, which is much more fluid than

47

you recognize. It can, for instance, flow both forward and backward under certain circumstances. This occurs only when the right preparations are made—a space must be cleared into which the essence of time is encouraged to flow.

"In part this is why we perceive time differently from you. It appears to flow more slowly in our world, though in fact it is moving at exactly the same time as in your realm. This is a paradox that I am unable to explain more fully. Nor is it necessary for you to know it at the present time. Indeed, it is far more important for you to realize that time has made you its slave in your world. If you are to move on, you must free yourself from this tyranny. Remind yourself daily that you are not the slave of time, that you can be free of it and that when you do so it will begin to stretch. This is not simply a matter of ceasing to count the divisions of time that are so much a part of your lives; rather it is a matter of stepping outside of the stream, watching it and being part of it yet no longer caught in its current. This is not as hard as it may seem. With practice you can begin, slowly at first, to step aside, to observe the flow of time. When you are able to perceive it as a fluid motion you may even learn to reverse the flow as we have done for many of your ages."

My next question was one that David Spangler had asked: did the Sidhe think of themselves as incarnated beings in the same way as we think of ourselves?

"If by incarnation you mean birth into the solidity of the world, then the answer is yes. When I spoke of our coming from the earth I meant that we emerged as did you from a state of ancient being into what we may call life. I am uncertain of the exact process by which your race emerged and how it has evolved—despite the fact that we have observed you for many ages.

"Perhaps it is that we both developed but at different rates. There is also the idea that you possess of losing the original purity of your creation and becoming somehow lessened. This did not occur to us. We are now as we were long ago. Our knowledge of ourselves is the same despite the fact that we have evolved in other ways."

"You speak of knowledge; do you have a concept of intelligence?"

"If I understand the question correctly, I would say that we are the sum of what we know. The knowledge of the world and the earth and the energies that flow through it defines us. Because we are ancient we have had time to study the things that move us forward. We are not static even though we move slowly. Our minds are subtle and quick but we step aside from this stream as from time, seeking always to develop the marriage of spirit with thought.

"Our evolution has been very different from yours. Where you have followed the path of the machines upon which you now depend, we chose not to follow that path but to spend our time seeking to develop other skills. Your race has called our ability "magic," but in truth it is no more magical than anything you have achieved. It is simply a different way of working. Thus, when we want to travel between one place and another we have only to dissolve our essence and reconstitute it where we wish to be. At the same time we have never truly left the place where we were, we simply sent part of our consciousness to that other place.

"Our ability to create a harmonious link with other aspects of life gives us the ability to do many things that seem magical to your kind. Yet you also could learn these things. They are subtle to be sure, but with time and practice they may be learned as any skill may be learned."

Again I asked for a deeper definition of these ideas.

"Consider for a moment, as I have already said, that everything has Spirit. You have Spirit. Stones have Spirit. The very air has Spirit. Thus, if the spirit within you can speak to the spirit within another, then you can create a link that enables you to combine the two within one. In this way you can bring about changes that are very subtle. You could, for example, change your form by establishing a link with the spirit of a creature.

"So long as it was willing to sustain the exchange between you, you would become the creature and the creature would, in a certain sense, become you. It is a matter of overcoming otherness. The identity which we all possess, Sidhe, animal, humankind, is only a matter of outer form. The reality of Spirit is much deeper and more constant, since it does not require form of itself. This is the importance of reestablishing contact between yourselves and the spirit within everything. Once you have reconnected your own scattered selves this should be a natural outcome."

"So you are saying that what we call "magic" is the manipulation of spirit?"

"Not manipulation. We are all part of a process that has no end—though I understand that this may be a difficult concept for your kind, who see yourselves as finite beings. Part of the process is to establish the deepest possible link between all things, all aspects of life.

"When this occurs, it occurs naturally, and the cooperation between each aspect of Spirit is such that there is no manipulation involved. You might wish to raise a heavy object such as a stone. To do so you need the agreement of the stone and the fellowship of the stone with your own spirit. Together, in harmony, the stone may then be moved. In this sense all things that are incarnate are part of the whole—many among your kind have already recognized this, but have been unable to move to the next stage. Once the understanding of this relationship is truly in place, you must be ready to move forward by applying the knowledge to your lives."

"How can we do that?"

"I am aware that this is a difficult thing for you to grasp. Try to think of everything around you as sharing in a larger state of being that is all inclusive. This does not mean that you have no individual reality, any more than it means this for us. Simply, it gives us both access to a level of reality that is different from the one you experience daily. One of your wise men said that all form was illusion and in some way he was right. The outer shape assumed by all beings at the moment of incarnation is far more subtle than is generally understood by your race.

"Thus, before you enter the world, you have already taken on the form you will wear during your lifetime. This form continues like an echo even after Spirit has returned to its point of origin. But this form is not the true nature of the being who inhabits it. That passes on to other things."

This was so exciting that I burst out with a question that I had already intended to ask. Were the Sidhe talking about reincarnation?

"In a certain sense that would be the name you have for what I am referring to. For us it is different, for we are so long-lived that few of us have experienced this. Yet we believe that Spirit continues when the envelope of form is discarded. Some there are who have returned to us and spoke more of these things. Indeed we are not deathless, but death is simply a small change in our relationship with the world as we see it. So, in a certain sense, we do not know death, merely the change from one state to another.

"But there is much here that we do not understand. We are not all-knowing, we are simply wise. We believe that our destiny is somehow linked with yours, but we do not know exactly how. Many ages have passed and we have lived side by side in the world with scarcely any contact. Your stories of us are strange and seem to misrepresent us so that we are frightening. Yet some of our kind have walked in your world, and those of your kind who are able to see have visited us. The reason I am speaking to you now is because we believe the time is approaching when you will perceive us around you. In that

51

moment there will be a great shift in the flow of Spirit, so that it is vital that you understand us and something of the nature of the life we share."

Some of the reading I had been doing prompted my next question. "Since you speak of the visits by both species to the realm of the other, I am curious about another aspect of the relationship that is said to exist between us. I have heard stories about contracts made between human and Sidhe, and how human men have loved Sidhe women and vice versa. Is there truth in this and if so what is the nature of such contracts?"

"Certainly it is true that our species have intermingled from time to time. In part this is because both our species are subject to the same kind of laws that result in a meeting of kind with kind. We, too, know the pangs of love and have been drawn to your species on occasion. We believe very strongly that one of the reasons for our existence here in this place is to learn about love, which we believe is a very misunderstood feeling. It is very needful that we learn to love wholeheartedly, both as individuals and as a race.

"We have seen so much hatred in your world, so much suffering caused by misguided affection or the denial of love. Yet we have been judged by you to be passionless, cold, reserved. This is far from the truth. Many of my people have shared love for ages without stinting. Among humankind it seems that love has become so fragmented into so many different channels that it has become weakened. You spoke of a contact and that indeed is one of the central aspects of love. It establishes a bond that is deeper than words, a bond that should endure and be honored despite the tests that it must undergo.

"Do not think that because we are of another kind we do not experience these things in ways very much the same as you. The purpose of love is to transcend the nature of human or Sidhe, to enable us to restore the damaged fibers of creation by presenting a harmonious image before the rest of creation.

"This is one of the things I referred to when I said that it was believed by many among us that there is a time coming when there will be greater communication between our two races. This may well be one of the means by which certain aspects of the disharmony within creation will be healed."

This was a theme that had come up before. I decided to ask, then and there, what we might do practically to bring about a healing of this disharmony.

"There are many things. One of them, of which I have already spoken, is to heal the fragmentation within your own spirits. This will lead to a greater recognition of the natural harmony within the universe, and this in turn will restore much of the damage that has been done to the very fabric of creation itself.

"Think for a moment that when the universe as we each know of it emerged, it was whole and complete, harmonious and sounding a resonant note. Each and every thing, every being and species uttered a sound that harmonized with each other. They formed a song that was more beautiful than we can imagine. But gradually, notes of disharmony crept into the song. There were those within every species, our own included, who became unable to recognize the note they produced. This led to greater and greater unbalance and disharmony. Within the shape of the universe many things came into being then that added to this disharmony. It could be said that one of the tasks of all species is to find their true note and sound it once again.

"This is in part the importance of love, for love is in all things, whether recognized or not, and where it dwells there is harmony of Spirit. If you were to spend more time contemplating this harmony you would be making a great step towards the state of which we believe you capable.

"Each day you should spend time considering your own note, the sound that would represent you if all things were seen as music. When you can utter that note perfectly, then you yourself will be perfect. It does not matter if at first the note sounds crude or even dissonant—in time it will change and you will hear the sound as it was meant to be heard. When all beings utter their note perfectly, then all of creation will once again be perfect. This is the second of the teachings we would offer you."

I thought about this for a moment. If all things had once existed in a state of harmony, what then, for example, was our proper relationship to animals?

"It is much deeper than you realize. Once you were much closer to all other species and understood them at a deeper level than now. They were your fellows, and when there was a need for any species to give their life for the survival of the other that was considered an appropriate thing. So, just as a human hunter might ask the spirit of the animal he hunted to give up its life so that he might live, so might the spirit of the animal ask the hunter's spirit to give up his life in turn.

"Thus was the harmony of things maintained. But in later time this was forgotten by your race, who believed, as they still believe, that they had a right to hunt animals to extinction. Curiously, it is those very creatures who have become guardians of the spirit realm. Often those of your kind who perceive the spirits perceive them as animals. What they do not understand is that the very creatures they drove to extinction are chief among those who hold the ways between the worlds."

In almost every book I had read about the fairy people it was said that they lived in a dimension generally known as the Otherworld. Now I asked if my visitor could say something more about the nature of this place—always assuming that was where they indeed lived.

"Our realm is not the Otherworld as you would understand it. As I have said, it is closely allied to your own realm. The Otherworld is a place where both races may journey and where they have often mingled in the past. In a sense I am in the Otherworld at this moment,

54

though I appear to be with you. This is possible because both places occupy adjacent spaces and these two spaces overlap. At this moment your world and mine are touching and thus you can see and hear me. The pattern of the Glyph acts like a magnet, pulling the two worlds closer together so that both may be perceived."

As I listened to this I began to wonder how our world looked to the Sidhe. In answer to this question my visitor answered:

"As both strange and familiar. In some ways it is very like our world, but everything in your world seems less brightly colored, less rich with life, than in ours. Thus when I look at a tree or a stone or a river in your world, I see something that looks a little like these things as they appear in our realm, but with the vitality taken from them. This was not always so, but we have observed a "fading" of your realm through the ages.

"This is not because the reality of things in either world is so very different, but rather it is that I see them through your eyes. Indeed it is one of the reasons that we come to you, in order that we may perceive the world as it appears to you, and so better understand you. But your perception is very clouded. Indeed, one of the things that we wish to teach you is to learn to perceive your world as it truly is."

I thought back to that day in the park and the wonderful experience of feeling the essence of the tree. As though he could indeed hear my thoughts, my visitor continued:

"It is partly a matter of not trusting the first impressions sent to you by your senses. If you distrust these, you are forced to look again. If you look again, you see more deeply. Each time you do this you will see more. There is a far greater range of color and texture than you seem to be aware of. The same is true of sound. Your ears are clogged as are your eyes by too many needless things. By seeing and hearing more, you see and hear less. This may seem a paradox of what I said about the need to see deeper, but in truth it is not. It is part of the whole.

"Just as you need to see more deeply, so also do you need to exclude the distracting falseness of certain images, certain sounds. When your eyes and ears are full, what do you really see or hear? The same is true of all of the senses. You must try to use all your senses more selectively and more deeply. Work to exclude the brash and futile things that clutter your life and you will begin once more to appreciate the true nature of the world around you. This is another part of the restitution of your scattered selves. The senses, too, are windows upon the spirit. When they are truly clear, you will experience everything more deeply."

This last statement triggered another question, one that had been hovering near the front of my mind for several days. I said: "There's a theory I have heard about that the fairy people might be responsible for the crop circle phenomena. Others have declared them to be fakes. Can you comment on that?"

"These things that you refer to are not of Sidhe origin, though we are certainly aware of them. Essentially, we believe they have come into being spontaneously, and that they are an attempt to enter into a kind of dialogue with you. Not exactly as we do now, but in a broader sense. Some, indeed, have been made by others of your race out of a wish to be part of the inner impulse that has brought these things into being. They are indeed glyphs much like the one you are now working with."

"I'm not sure I understand. How can these glyphs happen spontaneously? Who is actually causing them?"

"They are not caused by any one person or persons, despite the participation of some among you. Rather they are an expression of the most ancient forces contained in the Earth. You might say they are the Earth's way of communicating with you. They are an attempt to express concepts in ways that you will understand —hence they take forms that are familiar to you. It is once again a question of your consciousness interpreting what might otherwise be seen as abstract. Yet they express deep knowledge, shapes and patterns which are part of creation's ancient forming.

"It is too soon yet to see whether they will have the effect that is hoped for. Too many doubt them at the present time, or are concerned with the method of their creation. Yet if you were to draw out these glyphs and study them as you have the glyph by which we are able to communicate, you would find that they could open new depths of understanding the natural world, and of the mystery that sleeps in the earth."

"That is wonderful. Can you say more?"

"Think of it in this way. The Earth on which you walk is more ancient than any of us. It has existed for many ages and it will almost certainly exist when all other life is drained from it. There are great energies and forces hidden deep within the land itself. Some understanding of this has been possessed by your race for centuries—the simplest level of knowledge enables you to farm and harvest crops. Yet there are deeper levels that will only be revealed to you when you are able to enter into a deeper communion with all life. Next time you are out in the natural world, try to place yourself into a more receptive state, so that you can be aware of these things."

I put one more question, which though it seemed a minor one, had been nagging at me for days. If the Sidhe had been on earth for so much longer than us, and if the name by which they were known was in the Gaelic language, what had they been called before that? Did they, in fact, have a name for themselves? My visitor seemed amused.

"What a very human question that is. We do indeed have a name for ourselves—which I will not utter any more than my own name, for neither is needed here. We chose to call ourselves by the name that we now use because it is of recent origin and one that still has meaning for your kind. In the same way we make use of the Glyph though it was carved many ages before the race you call Celts came to this land. In each case the use of these things is sanctioned by its familiarity to you and your kind."

This particular dialogue ended here, but I could not forget the words of my visitor about the Earth's latent energies.

A few days later I went to visit friends in the depths of Wiltshire. Pat and Tom Croom lived in a small house at the end of a long lane. On every side was a mixture of fields and open pastureland. It was our habit to go for digestive walks in the evening, usually in companionable silence, and on this occasion as we ambled across the broad undulations of the land I let my mind sink into a meditative state. From there I began to think about the land beneath me, the nature of the earth on which I walked, where generations of people had walked before me.

At first I felt nothing, then—my feet began to tingle! It was exactly as though every step I took called forth a response from the earth. It was a very strange feeling, and I almost snapped back to a normal state of perception. But with a little effort I retained my meditative state and let my mind sink deeper into itself. I focused again on the earth and this time felt what I can only describe as a sense of communion with the land. I realized that every grain of soil, every stone and root beneath me was somehow connected. Even as I walked by the side of my friends along the barely visible track way in Wiltshire, I was simultaneously walking on every other piece of earth within a radius of several miles! It was a very odd feeling, and I realized also that if I could sustain it I could probably extend the radius much further.

Beyond this, I suspected that if I was really practiced at this kind of deep awareness, I would be able, somehow, to feel the presence of those who had walked there before me: people and animals, everything that was part of the web of creation. The earth where I walked was truly part of something much bigger, that totality which ecologists such as James Lovelock have called Gaia, after the Greek goddess, thereby indicating that the planet itself is a living being—something that the Sidhe seemed also to believe.

The experience probably lasted only a moment. Then I was back in my normal state of consciousness. Tom pointed out a hovering kite far above us and my contact with the earth shifted with my attention. But the feeling remained with me—is with me now as I write. More completely than anything I had read about such things, this experience taught me the reality of being part of the world I lived on. I do not think I will ever walk again on the earth without being aware of the deep connection that exists between it and us. I had learned another valuable lesson from the Sidhe.

Chapter Six

The Journey

"You have within you the seeds of great
distinction and unutterable beauty"

At this stage I had begun to review the preceding conversations, and to discuss them further with David Spangler. Some of what my visitor from the Sidhe had said left me with a feeling of negativity regarding their picture of humanity. One day, on a brief visit to London, as I was sitting on a bus, I looked out of the window at the whirlwind bustle of humanity thronging the streets. Everything seemed at once dirty and exhausted, and I found myself wondering why we had bothered to propel ourselves so far along the evolutionary road if we could manage nothing better than this. The feeling that overcame me then was dark and disturbing. Generally I have what I can only describe as fairly warm feelings towards my fellow men and women. Now I found myself questioning that, looking at the inhabitants of the city as though they were stamped with what the English prophetic poet William Blake called, "marks of weal and marks of woe."

When I got home that night I telephoned David and told him what I had experienced.

"This is what I was concerned about when I said the communications were a bit negative. So many of the things like this I've read since the 1950s have expressed a similar sort of dissatisfaction. It's very easy to see such things as an expression of the recipient's own feelings."

"But I don't feel particularly dissatisfied with my life," I answered.

"I know that," said David with a laugh. "Which is why I think you should ask your communicator what he thinks about this."

The idea seemed a good one, and when I had rung off I sat down at once before the Glyph and put this very question. I did so with some hesitation, wondering what sort of answer I would get; but my visitor's response was measured, warm and informative.

"It is certainly not our wish to cause such feelings. As I said when we first spoke together, we are an ancient race who has observed you for many years. We have not always liked what we saw—yet for every act of darkness, we have seen an act of light. Through the making of music and the creation of art, as well as through acts of kindness and generosity, you have expressed a fullness of Spirit that in every way equals any we have seen.

"The main reason for our contacting you at this time is because we have seen the potential you possess and because it would give us joy to see that more fully expressed. It would indeed not be worthy of us if we were simply to offer praise and assurance that you had already achieved all that you might. This would be false indeed and very far from the truth. You have within you the seeds of great distinction and unutterable beauty. Our fear is that you will not achieve this unaided, and though we cannot (nor would we wish) to impose our will upon you, we are able to offer guidance to help you take the next steps upon your road of development."

"A number of writings have appeared whose authors claimed to have received them from beings said to be superior to us," I said, thinking of the tidal wash of channeled books published in the past decade. "Many were critical but had little by way of constructive answers to these things." My communicator's reply was patient.

"That may be so. But I would not be here if I bore your kind anything but goodwill. There are indeed those among us who feel ill disposed towards your race—who look with disfavor on your path— but many, such as I, believe that because we share the very nature of creation, we are in a certain sense brethren. Our evolution has been different, and we have followed a different path from yours, but we are in truth not so far removed from you. Certainly we do not claim superiority. It is simply that we have moved further on a different path than you, and thus have received a different view of things.

"My own feeling towards your race is that of one who seeks to help you find the way to a fuller and deeper expression of incarnation. In time, there may even be a reversal of roles—we may need your help. We are certainly not perfect (perhaps neither race can ever be); in our own way we seek to evolve just as do you. It is my belief that we shall do so mutually as two species who are both on a journey."

"How would you describe that journey?" I asked.

"In the past—a time so distant that even we look upon it as ancient—it was said that a day would come when we would be unable to change, and that this changeless state would become a burden to us. We believe that time has now come. We have not evolved significantly for many ages as you would number them—yet we feel the need to do so.

"Your own race is also at a crossroad. You have come far since the days when you were Newcomers to these shores—and you have traveled so fast that you have become out of step with the rest of creation. It is as though you have left behind certain aspects of yourselves and certain parts that could be developed further. In your own lifetime you have seen a great increase in interest of spiritual matters—yet the effect of this has only been to lose focus—as though the very plenitude of spiritual paths has weakened your resolve to discover the things that remain hidden.

"Among the greatest gifts we have observed in your race is the desire to know and to explore. This hunger has propelled you far along the path of the day and the path of the night. Hence, your journey is indeed one of exploration, not only in time and space, but in the dimensions of Spirit. If I said to you that our two races, human and Sidhe, were on a parallel way, that our journey was in pursuit of similar goals, how would you respond?"

Rather nonplussed, I answered that I could not see how this might be, given the differences in our beings. He answered:

"Yet, is the disparity so great as you suggest? We may be formed in a different way (for this is not truly how I appear) and our nature may be different, but we are both seeking the same things—the answer to our presence in this universe. You are not alone in asking such questions. We, too, are concerned to know why and how we are as we are—in this way we walk a similar path, and it is one on which the sharing gives a unique opportunity to learn—for both of us!"

I was rather stunned by this. All I could think to say was, "You said you don't look the way I see you. What do you look like?"

"I cannot truly show you. Not because I do not wish to, but because your senses are not attuned to see me as I truly am. Thus when I appeared to you at first, I took the form that your kind have often given us. It is as though you have a common pool of awareness and perception that presents you with certain pictures. Thus, if I showed you my world you would see things that your deeper mind told you to see. It is the same for me. This is itself of no importance, but it shows how careful we must both be in accepting the messages of our senses. For instance, I wonder if we see you as you truly are? Might not my sense be as programmed as yours? It would be easy to believe that our impression of your race is false, that we still perceive you as you were, rather than as you are now.

"But I believe, as do many others of the Sidhe, that though you have changed, and most profoundly, you are yet unchanged in certain ways. Thus we hope to encourage you to look more deeply at the potential that is within you. If, in directing your attention to this, it becomes necessary to touch upon matters that seem negative, that is how it must be."

At this point I felt as though I had been put firmly in my place. But I also felt I had been answered and that the intentions of the Sidhe were nothing but kindly towards us—even if they did see our shortcomings with rather more insight than we were given. Certainly, my visitor's comments on our inability to see anything we were not programmed to see seemed important, and I determined to follow this up at a later time.

After this it was two days before I had a chance to tune in again to my visitor from the Sidhe. When he appeared I began by asking a question concerning the relationship between the fairy race and ourselves. Specifically, I asked how we were related, and if so whether there was an aspect of the Sidhe within us and even an aspect of humanity within the Sidhe.

"The relationship between our two races is complex. I have said already that we emerged first upon this Earth. The Newcomers, as we called you, came many thousands of years after us. At first we tried to speak with you, but your response was either (as now) not to see us, or to be afraid or angry. There are stories still that speak of deaths in both our races, arising from this first meeting, but it is our belief that these were a result of misunderstandings rather than deliberate hostility.

"This is all so long ago that even we are not certain of it anymore. Whatever the truth, we decided to avoid your kind, and took to making ourselves less noticeable, until in the end you simply forgot about us for many hundreds of your years. Later, we tried again to make contact with your race as it evolved, but again we were met largely with fear and hostility (though there were those who saw and acknowledged us), and so took to hiding. Eventually, as I have told you, we withdrew beneath the earth, where we live still. Largely, we have never felt other than kindness towards your species with whom we share the world as we do with other animal life.

"Now, at certain times in this long history of our two species, there have been those who chose to leave the state of being in which we dwell and live with your kind. Those who have done so have found themselves growing old and meeting death as do you.

"In the same way, your kind have chosen to come and live in our world, giving up your gift of mortality to become one of us. We have already mentioned that there has been love between our kind and yours and that our blood has mingled. For many years we were uncertain that this could happen, but in the end it was proved that we indeed could mate, and there are those who share the blood of one and the other race. The effect of this has been to allow us a window of understanding upon your kind, and, we believe, a reciprocal effect with certain of you.

"Those whom you call seers have been those who were attuned to our nature and spirit. It is our belief that with time and willingness on both our parts we may each learn to know one another better. In this way, you may learn from us and we from you.

"Despite our differences there are relational ties between us; we are different families who occupy the same sphere of life, even though not in the same way. You might say that we lived at a different phase or pattern of being to each other, yet we believe that we are constituted similarly. Also, our reasons for incarnation are not always dissimilar."

Nothing I had heard so far had prepared me for this. I asked at once if my visitor could say more about these things.

"From what I understand, our tasks are somewhat different. For you, it is the completion of a work that has evolved with you, but which was present from the beginning. You will have heard many times that the nature of this work has to do with perfecting yourselves. This is only partly true. Indeed, it would be a good thing for all the worlds if you could achieve this, but there is more to it than that. For what you are also required to do is to perfect your relationship with other states of being.

"You might consider these as the states that exist before birth and after death—which are, incidentally, different. You will have heard that all living things proceed towards a final goal. This is true, but they do so at different rates. Thus, we move more slowly than you, yet cover greater distance as this is measured by time and space. Other orders of creation, plants, animals, the mineral worlds, are also evolving.

"Only when you are able to bring your understanding to bear upon these other orders, to put yourself once again in harmony with them, will your next stage—and theirs—take place. This is the reason it is so important for you to become re-harmonized with the rest of creation. As long as you exist out of phase, there is damage to the great web everywhere.

"We, too, feel this. The wounding of your world can be dangerous to our state of being also. For our worlds and our state of being are connected through the heart of the great web of all beings and all worlds. The place that you call the Otherworld, where both you and I stand in some sense at this moment, is a place through which all of creation flows. Thus, you might move from one world to the other most easily without ever leaving your own place. This form of traveling is easy enough to master. All you need is a glyph of each of the places to which you would journey—then, as you are doing now, you can focus upon them and move from your world to the other."

"But how can we get to these glyphs? I understand how I found the one that I am using to contact the Sidhe, but what of the others?"

"These will become available to you as you push the barriers that limit you further and further outward. At present, you can only travel to the edge of the boundaries you have imposed upon yourselves, the blinders of which I spoke earlier. These can be removed by what I would call dreaming awake, by letting go of your grip upon the reality that feeds your senses, and allowing yourself to move outward."

I knew that I had read about something like this before. I racked my brains for a moment and came up with what I thought was an answer. "This sounds a little like shamanic journeying?"

"It is similar, in that the same area of the mind is accessed when you undertake such traveling. It is really a matter of tuning out the distraction of your senses and allowing the impressions of other states of being to assert themselves. Paradoxically, this occurs when you are more attuned to your innermost organs of sense. When you are connected to the circuitry of the web, then you are able to enter that state in which you can move freely. With this will come access to the glyphs that lead between the worlds. With this also can come great healing for your race—and also for ours. Though you may find it difficult to understand, we also are damaged.

"This is something of which I may not speak of in any detail, since it concerns my race only. I speak of it now only to show you that we do not see ourselves as superior to you, but as companions on a continuing journey."

"When you speak of being damaged — is there nothing we can do to help you?"

"It may well be that there is. It has been said among our people that those of another race and kind will be on hand to aid us when we need it most. Also, it is well known among us that if all the chains of evolution are linked again, and all orders of creation move forward harmoniously as they are meant to, then the wounds in our own being will be lessened or even healed forever. It may well be that your race are the ones spoken of—though it seems to me that we are still far from this time. For the present, it is enough that we speak together in this way, and that we are able to show you some of the ways in which you might help your own development and thus perhaps, in time, help us. Do not forget that actions taken in your own realm may well have effects far wider than you realize. In the chain of being all things are related, and even those not seen by the perpetrators can bring darkness to other worlds."

I asked a question that had been intriguing me throughout this exchange. It was this: "If I understand you correctly, we could have access to other places as well as that where you dwell. Can you say more about these places, and those who live there?"

"There are indeed many other worlds. We have visited them often over the ages, and those who dwell there have visited us—and doubtless you also. These worlds are, perhaps, akin to different states of being as much as to actual places as you would understand them. Each one has its own inner state of being, its own echo, as it were. These states can, in certain circumstances, become linked in a way that permits dwellers in either place to cross into the next realm. It has been revealed to us that creation is many layered, and that we may pass from one level to another—though this is indeed too simple since there is no sense of up or down in these places. Thus you may speak of climbing to another realm, or of descending, but in truth it would be more accurate to say that we move between these states of being, these Otherworlds, without ever moving at all."

69

I was in a state of some excitement by now, and could not help asking if this kind of travel could take us even to the stars.

"In the sense that those distant places to which you refer are in effect no distance at all, the answer is yes. There are those like ourselves who travel through the many colored layers with ease, for since there is no time in these dimensions, distance also ceases to exist. I would be misleading you if I said that I do not fully understand these matters. Perhaps I should say that I do not possess the words to explain it.

"Imagine if you will that merely by wishing to do so you might walk in worlds more distant, as you measure distance, than any world upon which you have gazed. This is why we have spoken before to you of the importance of your imagination. This may become a vehicle for infinite travel and perception, once it is fully awakened and has been properly trained."

"This is incredibly exciting. How can we train ourselves to do such things?"

"It will take time. You must learn to free your consciousness, to allow your imaginative faculty to develop far beyond its present state. There are certain exercises that we will teach you. They are very simple, but very powerful and if used over a period of time will begin to develop that sleeping faculty. At first you will think this of no great importance, but I promise you that you will come to view them with other eyes in time."

"What are these exercises?"

"One we have given you already—the way to open your awareness to other states of being. The more this is practiced, the greater will be the response from the world around you. As a further extension of this, I would say this to you: pay attention to everything around you: to the flight of birds, the movement of clouds, the dance of leaves in the air. Listen to the song of the wind, the murmur of the

70

river, the sounds made by insects in the grass, bees on the wing, the chatter of crows and the barking of dogs. Wherever you are and wherever you go, listen and look—and remember. For in these things lie the pattern of all creation, of which you are a part. When you can hear the sound of a butterfly opening its wings, then you can hear the sounds of your own immortal being. Soon we shall offer other skills to you. For the moment, it is important that we continue this dialogue further, so that we have greater command of each other's lives and thoughts."

At this point the session ended for that day. But I was left with a deep and overwhelming sense of excitement. I knew, however, that I must somehow contain this, and putting thoughts of further exercises firmly from my mind, returned to other questions that had come up during the conversation and that I now noted for use the next day.

Chapter Seven

Relations

"We live in a world that is painted by ourselves
to appear as it seems most agreeable to us."

During the time when I had been gathering the information from my contact within the Sidhe, I had also been reading about other invisible or inner beings of this kind, including the nature spirits called devas, whose role, many now believe, is to minister to the needs of the Earth and to plant life in particular. At the beginning of the next session, I asked if these beings were known to the Sidhe and what they could tell me about them.

"Indeed, we do have knowledge of these beings. Our understanding is that they are projected by the beings of the plants as caretakers who minister to them in ways that they cannot do for themselves. In fact, they are like images of the spiritual reality of each plant. When a plant is healthy, it manifests a guardian and helper to care for it. When it is diseased or dying, it cannot do so. Hence the things that some among you have spoken of, that when there are these beings in place the life of the plant is extended outward and it grows larger or more productively. Trees, especially, have more than one of these guardians—we believe this is the origin of the creatures called "dryads" in your ancient time. We long ago established a harmonious connection with such beings, who give us the gifts of fruit and herbs and other good things that are essential to our survival."

"You actually eat then?" I felt foolish as I said this, yet somehow I had never imagined these rarefied beings actually taking in sustenance in the same way as ourselves. I felt a ripple of amusement from my visitor.

"Of course. Did you imagine that we did not? We, too, enjoy the fruits of the earth, though we do not eat meat—a strange and barbaric custom in many ways. We especially love to drink the juice of certain fruits—some of which grow only in our lands. There is nothing to equal the pleasure of fruit received from the hands of a guardian of the tree or bush in which such things grow. Yet we require less sustenance of any kind than you. We are so constituted that a small amount of any food lasts much longer than is the case with your race."

"When we last spoke you mentioned a multiplicity of worlds and those that inhabit them. I have been wondering whether it might be that the so-called 'aliens' we have heard so much about in recent times may be related to the beings you are aware of. Could this be true?"

"As I said before, there are many worlds of which we are aware and to which we have from time to time traveled. To us there is no great distinction between one or another, though they are very different in kind and those who inhabit them vary a great deal.

"To us all are inhabitants of Spirit, and Spirit itself chooses to manifest in different ways. There are certainly those among these other species who, like us, travel between the worlds and some must have been seen by your own kind. It is possible that these beings have been perceived in a certain way that has stamped them all so that all who followed the first-comers have been perceived by you as similar in appearance.

"I mentioned that you seem to be able to see us only in a certain way, hence my borrowing the appearance you now perceive. This has to do with the training of your senses that I mentioned before. Only when you have cast aside the preconceived images will you see things clearly—and this also is true of your own world.

"Imagine that you saw something long ago that you named a tree. Imagine now that this being no longer looks anything like what you first saw. How can you shift your mind until you can see the reality of the being called "tree?" In the same way, if you were able to perceive the reality of your own incarnation, you would perceive yourself in a very different way. Perhaps even your own outer image would change. This would be seen as an evolutionary step. But perhaps you have already taken that step and are simply unaware of it."

"If that is true, how can we begin to acknowledge such a change?"

"Firstly, by observing yourselves more closely. By this I mean that you should be more open to the patterns that have been emerging in your kind for the past hundred years. This is shown by the increased interest in all things of the Spirit, and the increasing dissatisfaction (among many) with the material possessions that have become so important to you.

"This feeling is not accidental, but only a part of the far greater changes that you are undergoing. You have begun to shrug off many of the chains of perception that have bound you, and the eternal gift of questioning, which is as important as your desire to explore, has begun to come forth ever more strongly.

"In addition, many of your race have begun to sense things beyond the range of everyday perception. Many more such degrees of awareness are manifest in you now than fifty of your years ago. If you observe yourselves ever more closely, these abilities will grow."

"But how can we do that?"

"You must have patience. If you spend a little time every day seeking to pierce the veils that surround you, reaching out with your senses to make contact with the web of being and with each other, you will experience an ever-increasing response from Spirit itself. Consider that you are holding a conversation at this moment with a being you cannot see or hear—as such things are judged by your kind—yet you see me and hear me in another way. Even if, as I am aware you occasionally think—you are only conversing with a part of yourself—even if this were true, you are still learning things that are buried very deeply in your awareness."

"Are you part of me?"

"In a certain sense, yes. But only in as much that we are all part of each other. So in my world there are those who seek to make contact with that part of them which might be termed human. But in another sense, we are quite separate, and I am not an aspect of your consciousness that has separated itself from your ordinary self.

"All that I am saying to you comes from the deep well of our wisdom, but it is also your wisdom as well—not simply because we choose to share it, but because you have yourselves begun to access it. This is what I mean by recognizing that part of yourself that has already moved on. Let me repeat: spend a few moments—as long as you can spare—seeking to transcend the bounds of what you would call your earthly consciousness. The results of this will be far greater than you might suppose.

"Begin by making yourself as calm and still as possible, then imagine that you are unwrapping layers of understanding that is no longer of use to you—slowly become aware of your eyes, of what they truly see. Try to focus upon things— begin with the natural world. Try to see beyond the surface of the earth and be aware of what is happening there. Give some time to this every day for a period of your weeks—perhaps six or eight. At the end of this time you will have begun to accustom your thoughts to operating in this way. After some time, the process will become second nature to you, and you will see more with each day that passes.

"This is the next of the exercises we promised to give you. Pursue it diligently and you will soon notice the changes that are already happening. Remember that these things are not new, but are part of your own evolution. We do not seek to interfere, simply to remind you of the possibility you already possess. It is the gift of our relationship to each other that we are able to share in the great gift of life, and to help each other to move further into the web of being."

"You said that we might not actually look the way we think we do. Can you tell me what we look like to you?"

"If we really attempt to see past the form you have given yourselves, you appear somewhat as clouds of dense matter. But in most instances we are content to see you as you appear to us when we communicate like this—which is largely as you see yourselves, save for an additional quality of your energetic basis which we are able to perceive since we are more closely connected to that aspect of you than to any other.

77

"It may well be that, indeed, neither you nor we have any true form, but that what we perceive is the action of our senses interpreting what is seen and felt within the sphere of our immediate being. We live in a world that is painted by ourselves to appear as it seems most agreeable to us. Is this after all not the same as the creation of works of art?"

"This is an idea that I think would seem uncomfortable to many of our race."

"Perhaps. Yet if you are to make the next step in the chain of being, you must at some point escape the confines that the appearance of things has put upon you. Once you become used to such concepts, a greater understanding of the true nature of being will gradually be revealed.

"Another way that you may begin this process —the fourth of the techniques we promised to teach you—is to train your dreaming mind to journey into the places between the worlds where you may become aware of other states of being. This will help you to a deeper understanding of your own state. You will have heard before that all of your kind dream, and indeed that you can teach yourself to remember these dreams.

"It is also possible to train your mind to journey through dream to other dimensions. Thus, when you prepare yourself for sleep, imagine for a moment that you are in a great cavern, larger than the place where we first met, and that there are many exits from this place. All is lit with gentle light that illumines everything so that there are no shadows. Choose one of the exits from the cavern and follow the passageway beyond wherever it leads as you sink into sleep. In many instances, you will see glyphs carved at the entrance to these tunnels— they are intended as reminders of where you go and of the place to which each tunnel may lead. We have used these ways for many ages to begin our own journeys."

"Is this, then, a real place?"

"It has a reality outside of the dream state, but its true value is in the place between realities that you enter as you dream. Think of it as a way of conducting your imaginary self towards the next step in the discovery of your evolutionary goal."

"Am I to understand from this that you also dream?"

"We have always dreamed, but learned long ago to make use of this faculty to take us where we wish to be. The dreaming self is a true emanation of Spirit. All created things dream, and it is in a sense their dreams that we perceive as part our reality."

"Isn't that the same as saying that all of life is a dream?"

"No. Rather, there are aspects of what both you and we call reality which are similar to the dream world to which we can travel while sleeping. This aspect of reality is a place of great richness, as though it were air rich in oxygen to breathe, which is beneficial.

"So, we are both able to grow and understand more deeply the true nature of the universe. Indeed, the Sidhe sleep only briefly, and therefore we rarely dream for long periods. Yet when we do so, our dreams are directed towards specific goals.

"This is something you, too, can learn to do. By practicing the entry into the cave—which has always been a potent image for you as we understand it—you will find that in time, you are able to develop this faculty to a greater degree."

"But what is the value of journeying to these other places, even in sleep?"

"The value is that it will help you to develop the ability to see beyond the narrow confines of your present consciousness. As you become more aware of your place in the great web of all things, so many of your present concerns will cease to have such a hold over you. Thus you will be able to move onward in your evolutionary phase and rejoin the harmony of the greater life. In addition to this, you will

79

encounter other races who also have things to teach you—though this is ultimately less important than your reharmonization with the rest of creation.

"Nor, lest you should think this, will you encounter beings of greater strength who might wish to do you harm. It is something that we have observed on our own journeys, that only those of similar evolutionary stage can encounter each other.

"Also, remember that in this dream state physical events do not occur. Your inner self can watch and learn and broaden its awareness, but no harm can come to you from this. I say this now because I am already aware that your next question would have been to do with this."

The last words were delivered with a smile so warm that any sting or sense of superiority was taken from them. I had only one further question to ask at this point. It was this: "What you have just told me suggests a governing set of principles that control the development of creation. Does this seem to be the case from your observance?"

"There is certainly a degree of organization in the universe. Without that it would cease to be—or so we have believed for many ages. We are not aware of any central principal, a being who might be called a Creator, in this. But then, all such images are subjective, are they not?

"We each perceive the universe uniquely, but when we are gathered together we see what our united consciousness wishes to see. Often then we give form to our seeing, and this in turn hardens into an image that is part of our consciousness from then onward.

"Thus, as I mentioned before, it is our belief that we do not always see ourselves as we truly are, but as we were before, our consciousness being unable to move forward quickly enough to match the development of Spirit. This remains a mystery, but it is one that we believe may soon be understood better, by both our races."

My communicant paused for a moment, and I thought our dialogue over for that time. But he continued briefly.

80

"You may remember that I spoke of the importance of ancestral wisdom. This is part of what I have been saying here. The way in which we perceive the universe is shaped by the memory of our ancestors—this is just as much so with us as with you. Perhaps even more so, since we do not record our history as you do, preferring to remember it deeply within ourselves. Yet the ancestors, both those who are of this plane and those who were never—as you call it—incarnated, are a common source for remembering all that has shaped us, all that has made us what we are.

"For you it is a matter of becoming aware of all that has been and of sensing all that will be. This may be difficult for you to understand, but if you turn inward upon your thoughts of the past and future, of the shape of time and the shape of the cosmos, I believe you will see the truth of this."

As he spoke, indeed as he began to fade from my sight, I had an experience that is still difficult to describe. It was as though I became aware of a vast throng of other beings—not the Sidhe this time, but of our own race, crowding round. I could not see them as well as I wished, but there was a sense of people from many other times, all linked in some way to each other—and to me.

I realized that this was what I had felt on other occasions; when I had visited certain ancient sites and felt what I described earlier as a sense that I might almost hear the words of those who had lived there. This time it was stronger than ever before. And I became aware of something else—these were not simply the people of the past, but of the future also, of our own future.

I'm still not sure how I knew this, but even now, as I recall the event, I can sense again the continuity of these beings. They were, as my visitor had said, much more than ancestors of family or blood—they were, in a sense The Ancestors, and they contained within them the memory of everything that had ever occurred and ever would occur. I have heard it said that time is circular, and I have no idea whether to believe that or not, but if what I saw and felt on that day is true, there is certainly a sense in which the past and the future—subjective states anyway, as the Sidhe had reminded me before—are somehow connected.

Whatever the truth, I felt profoundly moved and changed by that experience, and believe that wherever I go, whatever the shape or direction of my life, I shall always be aware of the presence of these beings who are so important to us now.

Chapter Eight

Companions

"All creation sang its own song and in so doing brought itself into being."

By this time I was bursting to try out the visualization technique suggested by the Sidhe—that of programming my mind to a waking dream in which I visited a cavern that was a nexus point between the worlds.

A few hours after my last recorded conversation I decided to try it for myself. I shut the door to my study; having first hung a "Do Not Disturb" notice on it. My family is used to this when I am working. Then I settled down in an upright chair (I wasn't certain whether I was supposed to actually fall asleep or not, but I didn't want to encourage it), and began to visualize a huge cavern with entrances and exits leading off in all directions. I began to wonder what kind of glyphs I might see there, and while I was still thinking about this I slipped from one state of consciousness to another and found myself in the cavern—which was truly vast—staring at an opening to one side of which was carved a roughly diamond-shaped image that seemed to stand out from the wall.

As I looked at this I felt a curious sensation, as though I was actually moving forward while at the same time remaining still. This lasted for maybe a moment, but at the end I found myself in a different place entirely!

A vast ocean lay before me, its waves lapping gently at my feet. As I stared out, shading my eyes against a bright, though diffuse light, I saw what looked like a small boat approaching across the calm surface of the water. As it drew nearer I saw that standing in it was a woman of great and unearthly beauty. I thought she looked a little like my Sidhe visitor, but I soon stopped thinking at all as she held out her hand to me and invited me to step into the boat. Of what happened next, I am still unsure. The boat moved away from the shore and sped out across the surface of the ocean. As it went the woman spoke with me. She talked of my life—of which she seemed well informed—and of my hopes and dreams for the future.

I must confess that I do not remember all that followed. Dim flashes of memory returned to me afterwards of visiting an island of great beauty and of walking there for a while, talking with the woman from the boat. Then, at some point, we were once again on the ocean, and in a while I was returned to where I had begun. A dark cave mouth opened before me and to one side was carved the diamond pattern I had seen before. The rest of the journey is vague, but I remember waking to find myself still seated in my chair, but filled with such a sense of boundless well-being that I am at a loss for words to describe it. The entire experience cannot have lasted more than fifteen or twenty minutes, yet to me it felt like hours or even days. I felt curiously light afterwards, and went for a walk in which I remember my feet seeming to glide across the ground.

Since that time, fragments of my dream voyage have surfaced at odd moments—once I stood before some shelves in a supermarket for nearly five minutes, seeing myself leaning over the side of the boat and looking down into clear water of unfathomable depths.

I have since been back to the cave again several times, and on each have found myself caught up in a miraculous adventure that has brought me a deeper awareness of myself and my world. This is not the place to write of these things, but it is an indication of the power of the Sidhe's instruction.

When I next spoke to my visitor, a few days after, I mentioned my experience and asked him if the place to which I had gone was known to him, and indeed if the woman I had met was one of the Sidhe.

"This place you describe is well known to us. We call it 'the shoreless sea' because none that we know of has ever reached the further side. We believe it to be a place between the worlds, perhaps a little like the firmament of stars in which this world hangs. As for the one whom you met there, she is not of our race, but again is known to us. In your terms of understanding she might be called a goddess, but however she chooses to be seen, she is a bearer of great wisdom—as you seem to have discovered already. Many others like her await your encounter in the worlds beyond this one. I encourage you to explore them as fully as you can. Only enlightenment can come of such voyages."

"Is this what all gods and goddesses are then—bearers of wisdom?"

"It is very much a matter of how each individual chooses to see such beings—and of how they choose to be seen by you. I have said that we possess the ability to change ourselves—these beings are older still than us and possess deeper abilities. When they communicate, they, too, must draw to some extent upon the information stored in the consciousness of your race, but sometimes they are able to break this mould see note and appear as they truly wish to be seen. For those who see them in this way, it is a rare gift, for they are of surpassing beauty."

"I am not certain how to ask this question, but I have noticed that in almost every instance where beings of this kind are encountered—indeed, those such as yourself—the information is nearly always pertinent to us. Are you—are they—so interested in our ways?" My visitor smiled at this.

"You are wondering if we are all a part of your own consciousness since we seem to have so much knowledge of you—but you forget that we have studied your kind for many ages. Your lives and your ways are of interest to us because of the way they affect our own lives. I have said before that your actions can affect us—even threaten us—though ultimately we believe that you will find your way to a deeper understanding.

"Thus there are many that are willing to help you—including these older ones whom you call gods. Your kind has spent so much time and concern over the nature of such beings that they form a large part of your inner world.

"We long ago integrated this kind of awareness of the nature of creation into our own selves. In some sense, you could say that we have included the gods within us, but this is a process that is too hard for me to speak of to you at this time. The day will come when you are able to understand these matters for yourselves, and then we shall speak of them some more.

"In the meantime, one of the things you must do is learn to think in a new way—or perhaps I should say, in a more ancient way. A long time ago your thought processes took a turn away from their true course. You began to place ideas in ranks so that they marched side by side as if they were soldiers. This you called logic. But, truly, you need to learn how to send your thoughts out in every direction at once, so that they relate to everything rather than to one or another aspect of what you call reason. Reason can be your greatest enemy when it demands that you cease to be open to other ways of thought. Thus, your determination to cut yourself off from the rest of the living world and become instead lost in the mechanisms of things, has placed you far from the true path of your advancement. Only by redirecting your conscious thought patterns into other avenues of freedom will you begin to enter the proper state of being that was always your destined course."

I felt more than a little overwhelmed by this, as well as by the experience of my dream-journey. For this reason I cut short my dialogue for that day, and once again work took me away from home—this time on a conference trip to Finland. There, I enjoyed several walks by the incomparable lakes and forests that crowd in around the city of Helsinki. Although the experience was not as direct or powerful as my earlier encounters with the natural world, it nevertheless served to reinforce the ever increasing sense of connection I felt towards my own environment.

This made me think again about the Sidhe and their relationship to their own world—and to ours. Despite the information I had already received regarding their history and connection with our own species, I still felt the need to go more deeply into this area. My visitor had referred to various aspects of this topic throughout our time together, but I had specific questions which I wanted to put.

So, when I returned home and had taken care of all the mail that had piled up on my desk while I was away, I settled myself once again before the Glyph pinned to my wall, and once my visitor had appeared, asked if he could tell me more, in general, about the way of life of the Sidhe and what, if any, beliefs they possessed.

"I will try to answer your questions, though these are large topics and perhaps of less importance than you suppose. As to our way of life, we are like you in that we spend much of our time studying the way in which the universe is constituted. We do not have what you call scientists—for we have no science in the true sense—but there are those who study the cosmos and try to understand its workings. Perhaps it might be better to say that the study of these matters is our science, and that a belief in the Spirit that informs all is at the heart of our spirituality.

"At one time we possessed a more complex set of beliefs, but these have become simplified over time, until now there is little remaining beyond these central concerns that I have mentioned.

"Once there were many tribes of our race with some difference in appearance—you might think of them as subspecies. The existence of these gave rise to many of your stories about us, and to a certain amount of confusion. Tales of fairy folk, of dwarves, goblins, sprites and suchlike, derive from our presence within your realm. As we withdrew further and deeper into the inner worlds, so we gradually simplified ourselves.

"This may be hard for you to understand, but it is as if your own racial types became increasingly blurred until you appeared outwardly as one people—for us we are the Sidhe, yet we are also many other beings. We have been able, by entering deeply into the matrix of creation, to reform ourselves, and to simplify ourselves genetically. This has been done from within. It has encouraged in us a more single-minded attention to our inner selves. It is likely that your race will follow this path in time to come, though this may not be for several thousand of your years."

"You're saying that you changed your appearance from within?"

"In effect, yes. That is why, with the passage of time in your world, the varieties of our kind grew less and were seen less often. It is rare now to hear of anyone seeing a gnome or a goblin unless those to whom we reveal ourselves choose to see us in one of these forms. Generally, we appear as you see us now, though we can take other forms also, as I have explained."

"What about the world in which you live? You said you could not show it to me, but can you describe it?"

"We live in a liquid world, a place of constant movement, a place of song. Much of our time is spent in the making of music—though for us it is more serious than a pleasant pastime, since it is part of our creative process in more than an abstract fashion. We have learned to create life through music, though our skills are limited when compared with the great song that we believe brought forth the universe."

"I think I have heard of this before. What interests me, though, is who you perceive as singing the song?"

"Not any one being, indeed not a number of beings. It is hard for me to describe this, but perhaps one might say that all creation sang its own song and in so doing brought itself into being? I do not have the words to describe this further."

"I'm fascinated by the notion that you live in a liquid world. How is this possible within the context of the universe—at least as we observe it?"

"You must remember that while we occupy the same space as your race, it is not constituted in the same way. At an elemental level our world is very different from yours, and we are able to exist there in a different state of being and are subject to very different laws than is your world. I did not mean that we live in water, but that the formation of our world is constantly in a fluid motion. We do have form, yet it is not a fixed form. This is why we have changed so little over the ages, save to simplify ourselves yet more in terms of character and type. It is also why we are able to pass through your world at every level, physically and spiritually, so that you are aware of us both in the realm of the senses and in that of Spirit."

I have to admit to some confusion at this point. As I struggled to record the answers to these questions, I became increasingly aware of the strain felt both by my communicator and by myself as we sought to maintain the contact.

It was as though, as we plunged deeper into the very nature and consistency of the Sidhe, our contact weakened. I can only attribute this either to my own lack of understanding (which gave rise to a good amount of frustration) or to the fact that, at some level, the worlds of Sidhe and human were like oil and water—they simply would not mix.

Feeling I could go no further with this I asked another question: "Your name I know means People of Peace. Do you have anything to say to us on how we might bring peace to our world?"

"I would say this to you. The true desire for peace must come from a deeper well than that of simple need or of the wish of one leader or tribe to become stronger than the other. We have observed your wars and your peace many times down the ages and none has ever seemed to be of endurance. You make war as easily as you make love, and you talk endlessly about the reasons for one or the other.

"This may sound unduly harsh, but it is simply an observance. I repeat that the need for peace must come from a deeper level, from the place where Spirit holds sway over the making of choices. It is our belief that if you were to convey this message to your leaders most would scoff at it. How many would be prepared to meditate and go inward to the place of the spirit to meet and discuss the terms of a settlement? Yet it is in this inner place that such terms should always be made."

Another question was already nudging at the edge of my mind as I listened to this. When my communicator fell silent, I asked: "When I hear you speak in this way it feels somehow different from other conversations we have had. Sometimes I feel that, while you appear always the same, in fact there is more than one of the Sidhe speaking to me?" My visitor smiled at this:

"There is a sense that you have been listening to all the Sidhe every time we have communicated. Though we are separate beings, we share in some ways a common area of thought. You might say our consciousness is linked, just as our two races are linked by the Great Web. Thus at times you have heard one of us speak and at others another. Yet we are all one in some ways, single and many at once."

"Is that something that might happen to us?"

"It is possible, though I believe your evolutionary thread is spinning differently. Much that I have told you has been to do with relationships to each other, to the environment in which you have your being, and to other races such as ourselves. In a sense, you are already linked to everything, and these links can only become stronger. But I do not believe that you will ever be joined as we are."

I now put another of the questions that has been nagging at my consciousness for some time: "You spoke before of the state of being before birth and after death as different. Can you add to this?"

"I did indeed say that the states of being before and after the period of life are different. This is because they are a continuing process. We each come from a place beyond, enter this realm we call the world, and depart from it to another place.

"We have journeyed there and have seen all three places. We are also certain that there are further states, both before and after those that we know of. We do not know what these are, but many among us believe that there are a number of gates through which we pass onward. The distance between the gates may be great—or it may be small. Yet it is certain to us that we do not progress by repetition—the process that you have termed reincarnation—but by a process that may well have no end. While we are engaged upon the journey, we have no sense of where it leads—even though we may tell ourselves this for the sake of reassurance, we cannot truly know until we arrive.

"Such, at least, is how we have perceived the process of being that both your race and ours call life.

"We believe it is this that makes you fearful of the states you call past and future, and that makes you reluctant to look at the present with clear sight. 'This was once,' you say; or 'That will be so in the future.' If you could but learn to say, 'This is how things are,' or, 'Thus they stay still,' you would begin to invite both the past and the future into the present, so that all would become a seamless web.

"The value of this is that the lessons and wisdom that are and were and will be are all present now. This is another of the crucial things which you must understand if you are to advance properly towards your true state of being."

At this point I began to feel that my conversations with the Sidhe were coming to a close. I'm not sure how I knew this, for nothing had been said, and I certainly felt that I had as many questions to ask as I had had at the beginning. I decided to grasp the nettle and ask, "I sense that our dialogue is reaching its conclusion. Is this true?"

"Indeed yes. The fluidity of our nature means that we shall not be able to hold this link between our worlds open for much longer.

"However, we would wish to share one further means of working on your consciousness before we go our ways. This concerns the opportunity to receive guidance and instruction from beings like ourselves who have the ability to walk with you far longer than us. Many of your teachers already instruct you in such matters. We would only seek to reinforce these teachings.

"I have spoken before of the Great Web that connects all life. It is vital that you learn how to make contact with that form that links us all. Indeed, there are many beings who live between the worlds, and that can pass easily between one and another.

"Many possess the ability to guide other races, such as your own, into the realm of Spirit as it manifests elsewhere. When you sit down and begin to attune yourself to the Web, either by way of the Glyph or by whatever method you prefer for inner attunement, soon you will become aware that there are those present who are not quite within sight, but who wish to become manifest. They can only do so through the shifting of your consciousness in the way that I have spoken of already. As your awareness shifts so they will become more solid seeming, though in fact they are like air to you that has taken form as have I for a brief time.

"Sometimes they may appear like animals, at others like beings you consider to be mythic. But you will recognize them from their intent, which will be felt in your consciousness like a gentle heat that passes between you. These beings mean only good towards you, and may not lie if asked their purpose. With them you may travel to many places within the Otherworld, which is, as you measure space, almost without limit. Once you are aware of these beings you may begin the process of exploring—as your nature will dictate to you— and in uncovering more of the hidden links between yourselves and the Web.

"Above all, I would say again what I have said throughout these dialogues: be reconnected to everything, end the state of fragmentation that exists within you and that is everywhere in your world. Only when this has happened will you be prepared to move on, to seize the opportunity to grow and develop to the point where you can once again take your rightful place in the greater whole.

"That is the heart of our message to your race. Only you can achieve this goal."

I needed to know one more thing before I said what I thought was to be goodbye to the Sidhe. I asked: "At the beginning of these conversations you mentioned a great disaster that might come upon us. Can you say more about that?"

"The disaster that threatens your race is one of increasing blindness. I do not mean that your eyes will cease to function, only that you will be less and less able to see the truth that surrounds you.

"Every part of your world is divided, fragmented, filled with opposition against itself. Every fragment strives with another for something they cannot reach—harmony. Yet, if your race learns to

95

reach beyond these divisions, these opposites, you will find that there is a pattern of wholeness that is indivisible and allows no fragmentation. You know this in yourselves even though you seldom own it. There is a deep reservoir of oneness beyond the divisive way you live. Seek that and you will discover the deep harmony that exists in all creation.

"I have spoken often about the need to reestablish contact with the harmony of the universe around you, to reconnect with those parts of your own inner self that you have neglected for many ages. If you do not do so there is a chance that your species will cease to develop at all, and you will simply become stuck in a backwater from which you cannot escape.

"This is not the purpose of your incarnation, any more than it is ours. We believe this can be averted, and we make no prediction of a dark tomorrow. It is simply our wish to alert you to the possibility, and to offer the ways of working that you have now received and that we hope will aid you in restoring yourselves to the harmony of the Web. If we are successful in this then we shall be content. If not, the sorrow we experience will be that of fellow travelers who see our companions being left behind."

Here my communicant paused for a moment, and I felt his regard for me like a warm glance. Then he said:

"Until the day when we greet you at the gates to our world, I bid you farewell."

With that he was gone, and my dialogues with the Sidhe ended, almost as abruptly as they had begun. I sat for a time staring at the Great Glyph, wondering why I suddenly felt sad and lonely, as though a dear friend had left me for good. I could scarcely believe that only a little more than a month had passed since I had first crawled into the mound of Gortnasheen and begun a new chapter in my life. Already I felt the many changes wrought in me by the communications I had received. My attitude to the world in which I lived was changed forever. Never again could I walk in the woods, or by the sea or even in the dusty streets of a city without being aware of the greater life that surrounded me.

I had, also, a new feeling of certainty and optimism about the future of my own race. After who knew how many thousands of years, we had made fresh contact with a race who had been here on this Earth far longer than us, and who still retained the wisdom and understanding of life that we had largely forgotten or neglected in the rush to develop ourselves. The Sidhe knew better than this, saw beyond the narrow windows of our world to a place of infinite beauty and vitality where, with but a few simple actions, and some very small steps, we also could be.

Chapter Nine

The Greater Harmony

"In truth you will cease to be observers at all
and become part of the thing you are looking
at."

Because of the nature of the communications from the Sidhe, I felt it necessary to record the exercises that my visitor passed on to me just as they were received—that is, often as part of a continuing dialogue. However, from the point of view of the reader, I thought it might be helpful to have them written out clearly and simply as separate entities in themselves. Hence, in this final chapter, I have extracted these specific teachings—six in all, including the use of the Great Glyph—that follow here set out for everyday use.

My communicator made it clear that it was a sustained and consistent use of these techniques that would bear fruit, and having worked with them now for some time, I can vouch for the changes they have begun to make in me—especially in the way I perceive the universe around me and of which I am a part.

Whether the use of these exercises can bring about the kind of evolutionary step described by the Sidhe is another matter, and one that only time will tell. But I present the core teachings of the Sidhe here for use by anyone and everyone, and in a sincere belief that they can only benefit us in the long run.

All six exercises are extremely simple in themselves. Yet, like many such things, they are also profound and can lead to the most extraordinary experiences. Only the use of these teachings can verify one way or the other the truth of what the Sidhe told me. Again, as with the dialogues reproduced above, it is up to the reader whether or not they find within them, as I most certainly have, access to a vital inner reality that touches everywhere on the world in which we live.

EXERCISE 1: THE GREAT GLYPH

It was made clear to me from the start that the use of the Great Glyph was not for me alone. Others could use it and were to be encouraged to do so. As with the rest of the Sidhe material, I was hesitant at first regarding the validity of offering this method of communication to the world. But again and again, my communicator assured me that no harm would come to those who used it, while knowledge of the kind I had myself received would be offered to those who sought such gifts with a true desire for self-fulfillment. "To those who approach these matters simply from idle curiosity or with uncertain motives, nothing will come of their use of the Glyph," my communicator stated when I asked about this.

Here, then, appears the Glyph exactly as I copied it from the chamber of Gortnasheen (redrawn for this book). It is suggested that you photocopy it or cut out the one on page 116, perhaps blowing it up if necessary, and pin it to a wall where you can see it easily from a comfortable chair. If you desire you might light two candles, placing one on either side of the picture. Then, seating yourself in your chair, study the Glyph for a while, allowing it to sink into your mind while stilling your thoughts. When you feel ready and sufficiently relaxed, close your eyes and follow wherever the Glyph leads. This may take a few attempts before you get anything, but persevere, especially if you are unused to meditation. It is a good idea to have a pen and paper ready to write down anything that comes to you. It is also worthwhile stating here that whatever you see or hear may bear little resemblance to my own communications. My understanding of the Sidhe's words give me to believe that each and every person perceives and understands things differently. So, if you find yourself speaking to a being who looks and sounds different from the being described by me, don't think this is an indication of failure. Keep working with the images that arise and follow where they lead.

EXERCISE 2: OPENING TO AWARENESS

So much of what my visitor had to say was concerned with new ways of looking, of really seeing. Implicit is the understanding that if we take the trouble to look past the surface of things, we shall see a great deal more. Such, at least, was my own experience when walking in a London park. Among the many statements, not really exercises in themselves, that my visitor made to me, the one that follows seems a perfect introduction to the second exercise.

"At the moment when you go out into nature, you see only the surface of things. Trees, grass, water, plants. Yet the reality of these things is far greater. Once you knew this. You can discover it again, if you truly wish. Next time you are outside, look around you. Try to see beyond the surface into the true nature of the things before you. Though you may find it difficult to do so at first, in time you will begin to see more and more. If you continue far enough and deeply enough you will even begin to communicate with the spirit within the things you are observing. In truth, you will cease to be observers at all, and become part of the thing you are looking at.

"Begin by making yourself as calm and still as possible, then imagine that you are unwrapping layers of understanding that are no longer of use to you—slowly become aware of your eyes, of what they truly see. Try to focus upon things—begin with the natural world. Try to see beyond the surface of the earth and be aware of what is happening there. Give some time to this every day for a period of your weeks—perhaps six or eight. At the end of this time you will have begun to accustom your thoughts to operating in this way. After some time, the process will become second nature to you and you will see more with each day that passes."

EXERCISE 3: PAYING ATTENTION

There is no doubt that everything my visitor from the Sidhe had to say related in one way or another to observing and attending to the world around us. In this third instruction—(hardly an exercise so much as an instruction to see everything in a particular way) this theme, when I followed it, came to the forefront and brought with it a deep sense of belonging to the universe.

"Pay attention to everything around you: to the flight of birds, the movement of clouds, and the dance of leaves in the air. Listen to the song of the wind, the murmur of the river, the sounds made by insects in the grass, bees on the wing, the chatter of crows and the barking of dogs. Wherever you are and wherever you go, listen and look—and remember. For in these things lies the pattern of all creation, of which you are a part. When you can hear the sound of a butterfly opening its wings, then you can hear the sounds of your own immortal being."

EXERCISE 4: DREAM JOURNEYS

The Sidhe several times spoke of the need for us to train our minds to enter states of being in which we could see more clearly. One of these was what he called, "Dreaming Awake," in which the sleeper (or maybe the day-dreamer?) programmed himself or herself to visit a certain place. The accompanying image of the cave is one that I have already found to be extremely powerful, as described in Chapter 7.

"When you prepare yourself for sleep, imagine for a moment that you are in a great cavern, larger than that at the place where we first met, and that there are many exits from this place. All is lit with gentle light that illumines everything so that there are no shadows. Choose one of the exits from the cavern and follow the passageway beyond wherever it leads as you sink into sleep. In many instances, you will see glyphs carved at the entrance to these tunnels—they are intended as pointers of where you may choose to go and indicators of the place to which each tunnel may lead. We have used these ways for many ages to begin our own journeys."

EXERCISE 5: THE NOTE OF PERFECTION

The Sidhe often seemed to speak in terms of harmony and sound, so that it was scarcely surprising to find that a particular emphasis was placed upon the idea of sounding a true note. Having tried this a number of times myself, I can vouch for the extraordinary enlivening effect that this simple action has upon those who perform it. Though I am by no means musical, I have found that after the first few toneless attempts, a far sweeter sound emerges—and with it a steadily growing sense of personal strength and self-awareness.

"Each day you should spend time considering your own note, the sound that would represent you if all things were seen as music. When you can utter that note perfectly, then you yourself will be perfect. It does not matter if at first the note sounds crude or even dissonant—in time it will change and you will hear the sound as it was meant to be heard. When all beings utter their note perfectly, then all of creation will once again be perfect."

EXERCISE 6: COMPANIONS ON THE JOURNEY

The final exercise given to me by the Sidhe seemed, in its own way, to hold out a promise of more discoveries. If, as my visitor has said, there are truly others out there who are willing to help us on our own journey, then an exciting future lies before us.

"Sit down and begin to attune yourself to the Web, either by way of the Glyph or by whatever method of inner attunement you are used to. Soon you will become aware that there are those present who are not quite within sight but who wish to become manifest. They can only do so through the shifting of your consciousness in the way that I have already spoken to you about. As your awareness shifts, so the beings will become more solid seeming (though in fact they are like air to you, which has taken form as have I, for a brief time).

"Sometimes they may appear like animals, at others like beings you consider to be mythic. But you will recognize them from their intent, which will be felt in your consciousness like a gentle heat that passes between you. These beings mean only good towards you, and may not lie if asked their purpose. With them you may travel to many places within the Otherworld, which is, as you measure space, almost without limit. Once you are aware of these beings you may begin the process of exploring—as your nature will dictate to you—and in uncovering more of the hidden links between yourselves and the Web."

Each of these six exercises has a great deal to offer, especially if followed for a period of several weeks. Slowly and steadily, you will begin to feel changes within you. Of one thing I am certain: the world will become a very different place to you as the mysterious and beautiful teachings of the Sidhe are revealed.

Postscript

I have not returned to the mound of Gortnasheen since that fateful day in 1998. Curiously, I have yet to learn of any media attention to the site. Keith Harris's own careful report has yet to appear in print, and I have seen no other published accounts of the discovery, or details of any subsequent excavation of the site after my own visit.

All of this has led me, more than once, to question my own experience there. Did I dream the whole thing? I do not think so. I have the presence of the Great Glyph pinned up above my desk as I write. I have the solid evidence of my senses, and my memories of my visitor are as vivid as ever.

Yet I wonder if, were I to go back to the mound, I would find the Glyph itself still carved on the wall, or whether it may have simply melted away once I had copied it. Ultimately, perhaps, it does not matter.

The Glyph has performed its function in linking me to the Sidhe. It is my belief that it will soon allow others to make that same link. I hope the message of the Sidhe will generate other questions in those who read this account—as many perhaps as those of my own that remained unanswered at the end of my dialogues with my visitor. And, I believe, answers will be forthcoming. I intend, one day, to make the return journey to Gortnasheen myself, in search of those answers.

Who knows what will happen if I do. Perhaps nothing. Perhaps everything. That is something that remains to be seen.

Further Reading

There is an extensive literature dealing with the history of the Sidhe and the many otherworldly beings that throng the lives and folk traditions of the people of Ireland. Many are obscure and contradictory — and many are contradicted by some of the statements made by the Sidhe in this book. I include the following brief list of books for the benefit of those who would like to know more — always with the understanding that the information thus gleaned will not always seem to equate with that received by myself in the preceding pages.

Coghlan, Ronan **Handbook of Fairies** Capal Bann Publishing, 1998

Keightley, Thomas **The Fairy Mythology** Wildwood House, 1981

Matthews, C. & J. **The Fairy Tale Reader** Aquarian Press, 1993

Matthews, J. **The Secret Lives of Elves and Faeries** Godsfield Press, 2005

Narvaez, Peter **The Good People** University Press of Kentucky, 1997

Spence, Lewis **The Fairy Tradition in Britain** Rider& Co, 1948

Spence, Lewis **British Fairy Origins** Aquarian Press, 1981

Stewart, R. J. **The Living World of Faery** Gothic Image Publishing, 1995

Stewart, R. J. **Robert Kirk: Walker Between Worlds** Element Books, 1990

Wentz, W.Y., Evans-Wentz, W. Y. **The Fairy Faith in Celtic Countries,** Oxford University Press, 1911

Yeats, W.B. **Irish Fairy & Folk-Tales,** Walter Scott, 1893

About the Author

John Matthews has written and compiled over sixty books on the Arthurian Legends, Wisdom and Grail Studies, as well as numerous short stories and a volume of poetry. He has devoted much of the past thirty years to the study of Arthurian Traditions and myth in general. His best known and most widely read works are *The Grail, Quest for Eternal Life, The Arthurian Tarot* (devised with his wife Caitlin) and *The Winter Solstice*, which won the Benjamin Franklin Award for 1999. He was recently guest editor of the journal *Arthuriana* and his book *Celtic Warrior Chiefs* was a New York Public Library recommended title for young people.

John has been involved in a number of media projects, as both an advisor and contributor, including the big budget movie *King Arthur*, produced by Jerry Bruckheimer and directed by Antoine Fuqua, due for release in 2004, on which he acted as an historical advisor. Much in demand as a speaker both in Europe and the United States, he has taught at (among others) the Temenos Academy in London, St Hilda's College, Oxford, and at the New York Open Centre, and at the University of Seattle in Washington. He has also worked in collaboration with the Joseph Campbell Foundation, with whom he continues to retain contact.

He is currently working on several new projects, including a study of Merlin. His eagerly awaited edition of Thomas Malory's masterpiece *Le Mort D'Arthur* appeared in 2002, and this year saw the publication of his history of wizards and a major divinatory pack, "The Green Man Tree Oracle." For more information visit Hallowquest.org.uk

Contact Details

The Foundation for Inspirational and Oracular Studies or FíOS, founded by Caitlín & John Matthews and Felicity Wombwell, is dedicated to shamanism and the oral and sacred arts. Each year the most inspiring exponents of living sacred traditions give practical courses. FíOS also offers a progressive program of shamanic training worldwide. For more details of events and courses, write to Caitlín Matthews *at BCM Hallowquest, London WC1N. 3XX, United Kingdom.* Membership of FíOS is currently (in 2004) £25 a year, giving members four issues of the *Hallowquest Newsletter* and discounts on special events. Send a sterling cheque for £25 (within UK) payable to Felicity Wombwell to the address above: overseas subscribers, please send a sterling bank draft for £35.

Hallowquest Newsletter: For details of forthcoming books and courses with Caitlín & John Matthews, send for their quarterly newsletter. Current subscription: £8 or 15 Euros (UK) or £16/$25 (World). Send sterling cheque payable to Caitlín Matthews or U.S. dollar bills (no foreign cheques please) to Caitlín Matthews, BCM Hallowquest, London WC1N 3XX, U.K. Alternatively, please see their website at www.Hallowquest.org.uk

About the Lorian Association

The Lorian Association is a not-for-profit educational organization. Its work is to help people bring the joy, healing, and blessing of their personal spirituality into their everyday lives. This spirituality unfolds out of their unique lives and relationships to Spirit, by whatever name or in whatever form that Spirit is recognized.

The Association offers several avenues for spiritual learning, development and participation. It has available a full range of face-to-face and online workshops and classes as well as long-term training programs for those interested in deepening into their unique, sovereign Self and Spirit.

Great Glyph Silver Charm

These silver charms are a wonderful way to be reminded of the wisdom of the Sidhe and our connection with them. They are approximately three quarters of an inch in diameter and retail for $9.00.

To order send the appropriate amount for the item(s) plus $1.00 shipping and packaging to Lorian Press, 2204 E. Grand Ave., Everett, WA 98201. Alternately, you may email info@lorian.org or visit www.lorian.org and click on bookstore.

Lorian Press

The Lorian Press is a private, for profit business which publishes works approved by the Lorian Association's board of directors. Current titles can be found on the Lorian website www.lorian.org and include this book and others as shown below.

David Spangler:

Manifestation: *Creating the life you love* - Card Deck and Manual
The Story Tree

Dorothy Maclean:

Call of the Trees
Seeds of Inspiration: *Deva Flower Messages*
Come Closer: *Messages from the God within*

Lee Irwin:

Alchemy of Soul: *The Art of Spiritual Transformation*

John Matthews:

A Constant Search for Wisdom
(in development - projected publication date November 2007)

R.J. Stewart:

Where Is Saint George?
(published by Starseed Publications of the same ownership as Lorian Press)

LaVergne, TN USA
24 November 2010
206020LV00004B/41/A

9 780936 878058